HOW NOT TO DAMAGE YOUR ADHD ADOLESCENT

Instead, Coach them Through their Turbulent Teens to Win at Life

Sarah Templeton

Gemini Publishing Ltd

www.ADHDLiberty.org
www.HeadstuffADHDTherapy.co.uk
www.SarahTempleton.org.uk

Illustrations by Sarah Scott Logos and Design

Cover design by Proactive Edge

Published 2023
by Gemini Publishing Ltd

ISBN: 978-1-7399588-3-1

WHAT READERS HAD TO SAY ABOUT SARAH'S FIRST BOOK:
HOW NOT TO MURDER YOUR ADHD KID – INSTEAD, LEARN HOW TO BE YOUR CHILD'S OWN ADHD COACH

So much helpful information to understand the way ADHD brains work ...

'... and how to reframe things to help your young person get the best out of life (and salvage your relationship and sanity along the way). Her years of experience (personal and professional) and clear passion to support those with ADHD are genuinely inspiring. I only wish that all parents/carers who suspect their child may be ADHD were given access to this book as early as possible.'

What an amazing book!!

'She hits the nail on the head, is straight-talking with everything and speaks from her own experience as well as being a fully qualified ADHD counsellor and coach. Sarah has made me feel empowered, starting today, on where to go from here to help both me and my son. A must-have for anyone wishing to learn the truth about ADHD.'

Do not underestimate what the right book can do for you and your family.

'This is the only book that gave us the tools to fight the system and confirm our instincts to enable us to speak the "language" of the specialist. It enables you to quantify your gut feelings and confirm you're not imagining things. It allowed us to set the scene and educate the school.

Our son was misdiagnosed privately three times. I was able to challenge the final diagnosis ONLY with the help of this book. We then obtained a QB test and he was confirmed as not only ADHD but extreme ADHD. We can now have the tools to support him and us, as a family, understand him.

I am so happy I was recommended this book and now finally, after six years, we can make a plan for our son. I absolutely know without this book we would not have been able to. I cried my way through talking to the pages. I used it to write all my notes and bullet point evidence as case studies.

Read it. Keep reading it. Use it as a constant reference. It's the best. Without a shadow of a doubt. There are simply not enough stars to give it or thanks to the author. She's changed our life and will make our son's life better.'

Wonderful book

'This book is beautifully written and straight to the point. I've recommended it to so many people and will continue to do so. Very informative and has taught me so much about parenting a child with ADHD.'

Excellent book

'The best book on ADHD I've found. So glad I found this book. Written by a counsellor with ADHD herself. So she not only understands ADHD but knows therapeutic methods to deal with all the traits. It's obvious how much experience she has working with hundreds of ADHD kids and her love and wanting the best for them shines through every page.'

Best book on ADHD

'Amazing book! Life changing! I started many books on the subject and it's the only one I have been able to finish. We can see it's an ADHDer who wrote it because it's never boring, goes straight to the point, hands on, and powerful at the same time. Eventually you'll come to understand your ADHDer and have a great relationship with him/her. I can already see the results. And it's nothing complicated, no complicated rewards system, just truly understanding the ADHD brain.'

Life-changing book

'The way Sarah has described ADHD is so relatable and yet practical. You just know she is on your side, not talking down to you or lecturing you (as we all know that doesn't help). It's a life-changing must-read, not just for ADHD parents, probably every parent and every human.'

WHAT READERS HAD TO SAY ABOUT SARAH'S BOOK FOR TEACHERS:
HOW NOT TO KILL THE SPIRIT IN ADHD KIDS – INSTEAD UNDERSTAND THEIR BRAINS AND TURBOCHARGE OUR FUTURE LEADERS & WINNERS

Every teacher should read this book!

'This is a user-friendly guide for teachers to understand the uniqueness of ADHD. It focuses on the strengths of ADHD and how teachers can harness them. Parents, recommend for your child's teacher. Schools, get one for your CPD library!'

Fantastic follow-up to the parents' book

'I have gifted one to my son's school and taken one to work. I will also be buying for teacher members of my family and friends. Carry on the education of others on ADHD brains, Sarah Templeton!!!'

What a fantastic book to read to get inside an ADHD brain.

'I can now get inside my son's head to know how he feels from day to day. I have now finished this book and will be passing it on to my son's teacher which will insure they will see my son in a different way. Teachers – please, PLEASE read this book'

Another fab book

'Read both of Templeton's books, one as a parent and one as a teacher. They are fab!! Please can you write a guide to help grownups next!'

I very much hope that this book becomes obligatory reading for teachers.

'It's about time people realised that most ADHD people are extremely successful in the entertainment industry, politics, sports, comedians, and they are far, far more than just naughty kids. They are kids with character. They are feisty. They want more. And that is what makes them, as Sarah says, "our leaders and winners".'

CONTENTS

DEDICATION

I'm dedicating this book to Anthony and my mum, who both left this world while I was writing this one.

Anthony was my third counselling client, 'Boy 3', in Aylesbury Young Offender Institute. He helped raise ADHD awareness inside prisons by getting officers to sit on his bed, forcing them to read the ADHD books I had sent him.

He was so passionate about keeping my teenage clients out of prison that he used to write personal letters to them, and his hard-hitting letters did change many a wayward teenager's life around.

Anthony, this book is for you. I love you millions, just like you told me you loved me millions in every letter, email and phone call. You cared so deeply about ADHD teenagers, and there are mums all over the country who are so thankful you took the time to write to their teens desperately trying to keep them on the straight and narrow.

And also, Mum, this one's for you. I know I was a nightmare teenager and you did your best to parent me with us both having zero knowledge I had ADHD. One of the last things you ever said to me was 'Do you think I could be ADHD too?' And yes, I now think you possibly were, but we left it too late to find out. Thank you for putting up with me and never giving up on US. We got there in the end.

1
HELLO

Welcome to what will hopefully be the start of you completely understanding your teenager's ADHD (Attention Deficit Hyperactivity Disorder) brain. You've probably picked up this book because you are either exasperated or perplexed by your own ADHD adolescent. Some of you might be at screaming point. Some might just be a bit confused as to what has changed since they were 8 years old and adorable.

However old they are and whatever stage you are at, I truly hope this book will give you a lot of insight. My aim is to help you understand everything that comes out of their mouth before the age of 20, and to limit the damage they do to you and your family but just as importantly – to themselves.

My name is Sarah and I was diagnosed with moderate-to-severe combined ADHD at the grand old age of 51. In my mid 50s, things became even more interesting when I was diagnosed with severe dyspraxia with 1% processing and 1% motor skills. I'd always known I was clumsy but really! One percent? Then also dyscalculia and sensory processing disorder. So for starters I have the same brain as, or a very similar one to, your ADHD teen.

Secondly, I'm a qualified coach and counsellor and have worked with literally thousands of ADHD teenagers. Some of these teenagers found themselves inside young offender units where I worked and counselled for over two years. My teenage clients in private practice and those behind bars ALL had one thing in common. I understood them. I got them. And I loved the bones of all of them.

Every single one of them felt misunderstood by either parents, teachers, prison officers or other 'authority' in their life. But I related to them because I was the same as them. I absolutely despised authority. Hated being told what to do. Always thought I knew best. Wanted everything my own way. Loved pushing boundaries, and although I managed to stay on the right side of the law, I could never judge teens who felt the same way as me but hadn't managed to.

I also had a VERY tempestuous relationship with my mother, who didn't know she was dealing with any of these neurodiversities and did her very best to bring me up. So if your teen is currently hating you – I'll be able to explain why and how you reverse that.

So firstly, thank you for buying this book. Parents who want to understand how their ADHD teenager's brains work have so much more of a chance of putting them on the right path in life. So pat yourself on the back for investing in your child's future and, in return, I promise you I will do my absolute best to help you understand and manage every nuance of their ADHD teenage brain.

2
READ IT – AND PASS IT ON!

I am passionate about people understanding ADHD teenagers for so many reasons. So I urge you to plough through this book and then pass it on to other people who are in your teenager's life. I don't want to put the fear of God into anybody, but things can go horribly wrong if you don't understand an ADHD teenager. At the very minimum, parents are going to have a difficult relationship with them as are their brothers or sisters. And that's the minimum.

Things can go more majorly wrong when they reach their early teens if they don't feel understood and supported. Battling an ADHD teenager is going to get you nowhere. Understanding their brain, how it works, what it needs and how to get the best out of it is always going to be the better option.

We will go into the ADHD traits in depth but, for now, know that their always-needing-something-more, adrenaline-seeking, risk-taking and thrill-seeking traits alone can get them involved in anything from criminal damage to stealing, drugs and alcohol from quite a scarily young age.

But forewarned is forearmed! The more you know about ADHD, the more you will be able to swerve these situations.

And at the same time as that, understanding everything you possibly can about the positives and the challenges of ADHD will allow you to steer your child towards a happy and successful adulthood – limiting the damage along the way.

3
WHY YOU CAN THROW TYPICAL PARENTING TECHNIQUES OUT THE WINDOW

I truly hope you haven't spent a lot of time going on standard parenting courses. I hope even more that CAMHS, teachers, social services or other professionals haven't forced you to go on standard parenting courses. If you've been on these, you will know that they don't touch the sides with your ADHD child.

Worse than that, they can actually do damage. Damage to you, feeling an abject failure because nothing seems to work with your child when it does with others. And damage to the child, who is being expected to magically transform themselves into a neurotypical child. It's just not going to happen.

If you're considering going on one of these courses, honestly save your money. There is nothing about traditional parenting that works with ADHD brains.

It really does boil down to the fact that an ADHD brain works differently to a non-ADHD brain or a 'neurotypical' brain as we call it. And everything I'm going to tell you in this book WILL work with your ADHD teenager.

So don't beat yourself up if you've been trying anything and everything parenting-technique wise and things seem to be going from bad to worse. That's very common before you understand exactly how an ADHD brain works and how to interact with it. With a bit of luck, once you start parenting ADHD-style, the transformation should be quite swift.

4
HOW THEY TURN OUT AS ADULTS IS IN YOUR HANDS. RIGHT NOW!

I don't mean because you are holding this book. I mean because they are teenagers! This really is a critical time for ADHD teenagers. Way more than neurotypical teenagers. Why?

Well let's start by clarifying just how much of a hormone-related condition ADHD is. Having given up science at the age of 13 due to a particularly ineffectual science teacher, you won't get the scientific explanation from me. However, I can tell you that ADHD is very much linked to dopamine in the brain.

As ALL teens hit puberty their hormones start cavorting round their body. Puberty can actually kick in as young as 9, but for most people it's around the age of 11 or 12. Now add in to that jumbled-up mix of changing hormones, ADHD. That's when life becomes really fun for parents. But if you think it's difficult for you, spare a thought for your poor teenager. Most likely infant and junior school were a breeze. They probably quite enjoyed it, had friends and life went quite nicely. But come senior school, puberty and racing hormones, life can ricochet off in lots of different directions. The particularly self-aware ones might even notice the change themselves.

I remember as a teenager, suddenly not liking anybody. Particularly my family who I found incredibly annoying. Apart from my father, who I now believe was ADHD himself and also I didn't live with him. From the age of 5, I only saw him once a fortnight which probably helped. But the rest of my family who I lived with, I could happily have thrown out the front door and never seen them again. They all irritated me intensely.

I'm told at around the age of 12, I developed an 'attitude'. It wasn't intentional. I didn't choose it. It just happened. Now I'm old enough and wise enough to know that this is because I had started puberty. But apparently I treated everybody as if they were an idiot, thought I knew best about everything, didn't understand why everything couldn't be my way (because that was the most sensible way) and was, allegedly, thoroughly obnoxious.

Knowing what I know now, and having worked with trillions of ADHD teenagers, I think my family came off extremely lightly. I never smoked, never took drugs, never skipped school, always did my homework, was in the school netball team for the whole four years I was at secondary school, won every speech competition I entered and was very active in the drama department. And managed to come out with a handful of O levels.

But – and it's a big but – I have worked with ADHD teenagers who have found themselves in some very serious predicaments and this is why I am thrilled you have bought this book. Because it's these teenagers I want to be sure you understand and I also want to help you keep them on the straight and narrow. This does not mean I want to make them boring. And it does not mean I want them to not enjoy their life. But it does mean I want to keep them away from skipping school and screwing up their education, keep them away from recreational drugs and petty crime, and most definitely keep them away from juvenile court and Young Offender Institutes.

Most diagnosed teenagers don't even google 'ADHD'. They're not interested. If anything they just want rid of it or to deny its existence. I don't think I've met one teenager in all the years who has been faintly interested in how their ADHD is affecting them, but they will happily sit there and tell you all the things they hate, how they are failing at school, what risk-taking and thrill-seeking activities they are getting up to and all the marvellous ways they've thought of to earn money without actually working.

So, because they aren't interested, I'm afraid it's down to you! They leave it to you to understand exactly how their brain works and to help them navigate their turbulent teens so they come out unscathed in their early 20s.

Once you've read and digested this book, you will be fully armed to handle everything your ADHD teenager might throw at you and fully prepared to limit any damage that will impact the rest of their life.

This might seem an impossible ask at the moment, but the most important thing is that they feel you are on their side. If you're currently at daggers drawn with your teenager, and communication is at a standstill, don't panic. Very soon you will understand exactly what is going on in their busy ADHD brain and you will be able to get them back on side.

You really do have a hugely important role to play in their life. I've worked with teenagers who have been arrested for all sorts of silly things, but with good, strong parents, they've all managed to swerve the nastiest of outcomes.

Your teenager might be acting like they aren't faintly interested in anything you have to say and their life is their problem not yours. But, believe me, you have a massive role to play in getting them through their teens and out the other side. And I'm going to help you.

5
DON'T UNDERESTIMATE THEM

I can't begin to tell you how important that statement is. For starters, never assume that because they have been thrown out of maths, never do any of their homework, haven't been near the bathroom for weeks and whiff, have no friends and seemingly no interest in life whatsoever, that this surely means they are destined for a life of unemployment and misery. It's just not true.

Much as schools have to emphasise the importance of education, passing exams and gaining qualifications, not doing so hasn't stopped one ADHD person ever.

So, tempting as it might be to badger your teen into doing homework and fitting into that square box the school wants them to, if they just can't, or they just won't, then don't keep flogging a dead horse. Accept that your teen is going to do things differently and that can still mean they become phenomenally successful in life.

Your role in this is huge. Each individual child's ADHD is so unique that it is going to be up to you to liaise with and represent them at school. No teacher, however well-trained, is going to understand your child's unique ADHD traits, severities and coexisting conditions.

Do bear in mind that, especially with boys, ADHD kids can be up to 30% less mature than their peers. So your 15-year-old may well be acting like a 12-year-old and his teacher will not understand why unless you explain this to them.

Critically, if an ADHD brain doesn't like a subject, or a teacher, or a particular classroom, there is very little that you're going to be able to do to make that right for them. With me, it was science and geography. I hated the subjects, the teachers and the classrooms. So I gave them both up at 13. Because in those ancient days you were allowed to. Nothing much has changed really, and if your child has an ADHD diagnosis, then you can negotiate with the school to drop subjects that really do not interest them and allow them to focus on the ones that they are interested in or passionate about.

If you remain on their side at all times, trying to see things from their point of view, you won't go far wrong. Always make it very clear that you want the very best for them and you know that sometimes their ADHD makes fitting into that school square box, not so easy. But if you and they are on the same side, always with the goal of getting them the qualifications they actually need for the college/university/career they want, with a lot of confidence and by using the phrase 'reasonable adjustments' frequently, you can get that taken seriously by their school.

I've worked with parents who have been absolutely at desperation point with their teenagers. Terrified for their futures. Quite sure they are going to carry on refusing to work, refusing to hand in homework, refusing to take their GCSEs seriously and doing silly, petty crimes that get the police involved. These parents are often run ragged and exhausted from trying to do the very best for their teen but everything they do to help seems to push the teenager further away. Whatever they do for them seems to annoy them. They don't seem to be able to do right for doing wrong and they are terrified for the child's future.

Luckily, I know exactly why that is and exactly what you can do about it. And all the answers are in this book!

Throughout the book, I'm going to give you real-life examples of when things were going very wrong, but then with the tiniest of tweaks, started to go very right. I'll give you lots of tips about working therapeutically with your child and coaching them without them even realising it.

I very much hope to be able to work through you, so your teen can understand themselves better. To like themselves much more. To have higher self-esteem, to know who they are and where they want to go in the world.

And for you not to have a nervous breakdown making that happen!

6
THEY ARE DEALING WITH A LOT

Everybody knows it's difficult to be a teenager. When you add ADHD into the mix it gets a whole lot more difficult. Primarily because ADHD is a hormone-connected condition and we all know what happens to hormones during puberty. If it's hairy and scary for any teenager, getting through puberty and out the other side is strewn with more issues and obstacles when you are dealing with ADHD at the same time.

Having worked with thousands of ADHD teenagers I know their main issue is that nobody understands them. Nobody gets the way their brain works and thinks and the subsequent behaviour. This can lead to huge frustration and irritation, especially with people in authority who expect them to put their ADHD traits to one side and behave just like everybody else. This is absolutely impossible. They only have one brain and it's an ADHD one.

At best this can lead to having 'attitude' which was me right the way through puberty, biting the head off anybody who dared talk to me!

At worst, the seriously misunderstood can end up rebelling in all sorts of different and dangerous ways.

Teens who are diagnosed with ADHD nearly always assume this makes them less able than others. They might be labelled SEN – special educational needs – at school and treated as if they are less able than their peers. This is the first thing you need to stamp out. They are at least equal to their peers, if not more able to achieve in life. It's no coincidence that three quarters of Hollywood, approximately nine out of ten top comedians, the most highly-decorated Olympians and (they say) ALL entrepreneurs are ADHD. But nobody mentions this to teenagers while parents and teachers are busy worrying about their attitude! It's this very 'screw you' attitude that is going to make them successful in life. They just haven't managed to hone it to be socially acceptable as they fumble and stumble through puberty.

A lot of teenagers receiving their ADHD diagnosis automatically think they are doomed to fail at life. That they are mentally ill or mentally sick. That they have a disorder, and they won't ever fit in, have friends or be in successful relationships. This is 100% absolutely NOT TRUE. I'm going to give you the tools in this book to help your teenager understand exactly what strengths, drive and passion their ADHD brings and for them, and you, to see themselves in a much more positive light.

7
SO – HOW ARE WE GOING TO DO THIS?

I'm going to assume you know nothing about ADHD. If you do then consider this revision! I'm going to explain exactly what ADHD is and what it isn't. I'll explain all the traits to you – some you probably know about but quite a few I suspect you won't.

I'm going to aim for you to actually enjoy these teenage years. And for your ADHD teenager to enjoy theirs as well.

In turn this will ensure any other children in the house have smoother journeys through childhood. I've worked with hundreds of families where the siblings would quite cheerfully have moved out to avoid the ADHD teen brother or sister! And If we get this right, you won't have the police knocking on your door when your ADHD child turns 13.

The only thing I'm going to ask of you is for you to trust me. Some of the things I'm going to suggest will have you smacking the book down on the table and shouting, 'over my dead body'. But please trust me! Because everything in this book works. It's been tried and tested with literally thousands of teenagers.

Every single one of these angry, churlish, outraged-by-anything, difficult-about-everything teenagers will become putty in your hands. It's honestly not hard. All you have to do is understand where they are coming from and how their brain thinks. And hey presto! Your life gets a whole lot easier.

Life is difficult when you are a teenager going through puberty anyway. If you add ADHD into that, it brings a whole raft of issues and challenges. All of which I will go into.

All the ADHD teenagers I've counselled, every single one of them has the exact same main complaint. Nobody understands them. Nobody understands their way of thinking, that their brain is different and subsequently their behaviour is different. This leaves most of them frustrated, annoyed, angry and with a festering sense of 'NOBODY being able to see things their way'. So helping you understand exactly what is going on in their head is top of my list.

Then we will go through all the scenarios your ADHD teenager will find themselves in and how best to manage each and every one – always limiting the damage possibilities!

My goal is to have you understanding their ADHD to such an extent that your home becomes harmonious, and your teenager has little or nothing to kick against. This leaves them free to focus on what really matters rather than battling wars that don't need to be fought.

And that all starts with you having a really good grasp of what ADHD actually is.

8
SO WHERE HAS THIS ADHD COME FROM THEN?

Now this might come as a surprise to some of you. ADHD is almost always hereditary. Yes, there are a very small percentage of people who acquire it through brain damage, but as you can imagine that percentage is thankfully very small. The vast majority of people who have ADHD have inherited it. So before we start sorting your teenager out, how about we look at where it came from!

This could be the first time you want to slam the book down on the table. But hang onto it and keep reading. You might be looking at your teenager, thinking, 'Dear God, I've never been as bad as him. What on earth are you talking about?' But just because your teenager is displaying some extreme behaviour, the like of which you would never entertain yourself, doesn't necessarily mean you haven't gifted them your own ADHD!

I've lost count of the hundreds of parents I've worked with who have looked at me absolutely horrified when I've told them that

ADHD is inherited. They start wildly flinging aunts and uncles and grandparents at me as 'possibilities' but, before the hour is out, we've always narrowed it down to either Mum or Dad, or both.

So let's have a crack at seeing if we can find which parent has passed on their genes, producing this ADHD teenager.

Any, all or a combination of these are indicators of undiagnosed ADHD in parents:

- **Addiction – and not only alcohol and drugs:** Addiction comes in many shapes and sizes. Are either of the parents addicted to chocolate, shopping, work, the gym/exercise, buying/shopping, pornography/promiscuous behaviour, gambling or hoarding?

- **Anxiety:** Anxiety and/or depression go hand-in-hand with ADHD. I've met many clients' mums who have said, 'Well I've been anxious all my life,' not realising that that is probably connected to undiagnosed ADHD.

- **Obesity:** If there's anybody in the family who has constantly struggled with their weight, failed miserably at diets, resorted to weight loss procedures and been to every slimming group on the planet – chances are this could be linked to compulsive eating due to undiagnosed ADHD.

- **Anger Problems:** Are there any relatives known for having a very short fuse, losing their temper and possibly even punching walls or being violent in some way? This is another indicator.

- **Offending:** If anybody has found themselves in trouble with the law, spent time in prison, especially if they ran into trouble as a teenager for things like stealing, criminal damage or affray – coming into contact with the police from a young age is another ADHD indicator.

If any of this is ringing bells with you personally, it might be worth you spending ten minutes doing an adult ADHD test online. There are numerous of these but a very reliable one is on my Headstuff ADHD Therapy website.

The reason I encourage you to find out where the ADHD has come from is because there are benefits to your ADHD teenager knowing that either or both their parents also have the condition. For starters it will make them feel less alone and less different. And secondly, it will help the parent/s to be diagnosed and probably medicated as this will change the relationship with your ADHD teenager for the better.

An undiagnosed ADHD parent is always going to clash and have more problems with a teenager than one who is diagnosed and on the right medication.

So jump on Google, find any one of the myriad of adult ADHD tests, and put anybody in the family who needs to be, on the path to diagnosis. It really will be life-changing for that individual and also greatly improve dynamics in the home.

9
THERE ARE THREE TYPES OF ADHD? WHO KNEW!

First off, it's critical you know which type of ADHD your teenager has. Because as I write this in 2023, the UK diagnoses ADHD in three main types. If you're lucky like me, you will be told which of the three types you have and what severity of it. So for example, I was diagnosed with moderate-to-severe combined ADHD. Nice and clear. What type and what severity. However, some paediatricians and psychiatrists usher you out the door with a diagnosis of ADHD, plain and simple. This really is not helpful. I can't begin to tell you the chasm of difference between the three sorts of ADHD.

My own family example is one of the best of these. My mother had me and my younger brother by two different ADHD fathers, one Combined and one Inattentive. I've inherited my father's Combined ADHD and my brother, eleven years later, inherited his father's

Inattentive ADHD. You really couldn't meet two more different people, but both of us are diagnosed ADHD. My Inattentive ADHD brother is largely silent, has social anxiety, doesn't enjoy meeting new people, and struggles with procrastination, lack of motivation and brain fog. Me on the other hand – you can't shut me up. I've always got plenty to say, I'm loud, I interrupt people terribly, was always the clown of the class, have far too much energy, love meeting strangers and I'm about as 'in your face' as it's possible to be.

So the first thing it's actually critical you know is which kind of ADHD your teen has. This is going to help them with their own sense of identity and it will help you focus more on the traits they are likely to be struggling with.

The three categories of ADHD are as follows:

1. **Hyperactive/Impulsive ADHD.** This is actually the smallest category of the three, and although some girls can have it, it is largely boys who do. These teenagers will be full of energy, wanting to do everything at great speed, probably talking very fast, doing everything to the max, so whether that's riding a bike at breakneck speed, go-karting very fast, bungee jumping from higher than anybody else – plus they will have oodles of energy, often don't need much sleep and are very adrenaline driven. They don't have the Inattentive traits, so there's not a lot of, if any, inattention, distraction, breaking things, damaging things, dropping things and forgetting things. It's all about speed and activity for this group.

2. **Inattentive ADHD.** This used to be known as Girls' ADHD, but that is absolute nonsense. In therapy I have met hundreds of male Inattentive ADHD clients, and calling it Girls' ADHD is quite offensive to them. People with this kind of ADHD tend to struggle most with inattention, distraction, procrastination, lack of motivation, brain fog, difficulty making decisions, being in large groups and are more prone to depression. This is the second largest of the categories.

3. **Combined ADHD.** This is by far and away the largest group. And the one that I'm in. This means that we have enough

traits from the other two categories to warrant a diagnosis of Combined. In the next section, you will see there are literally dozens of ADHD traits and the combination is different for everybody. It's not an exaggeration to say that in the ten years I've been working with ADHD clients, I've yet to meet two who are even faintly similar. That is because everybody has a different combination of traits and different severities of each of them. Not to mention different coexisting conditions – more on those later.

So if your teenager's paediatrician or psychiatrist hasn't been explicit in their diagnosis, do some research yourself online and find out which category your teenager falls into.

10
THE ADHD TRAITS NOBODY TOLD YOU ABOUT!

You may well have heard of hyperactivity, impulsivity, distraction and inattention. But did you know there are literally dozens of traits and 'ways of thinking' that are unique to ADHD brains?

Reading this section alone should give you a very good insight as to just how much your teenager is dealing with, as the vast majority of these traits apply to every ADHD person. Not all of them, because we are all affected differently, but it's highly likely your teenager is dealing with a good chunk of these traits and ways of thinking. Some of them are heightened or 'at their most extreme' during puberty, and I'll highlight these as we go through.

This is also a very good section to meander through with your teenager, so they can tell you which of these impact and impair them most. Some will already be very obvious to you, but loads of these ways of thinking may apply to your own teenager, and until they confirm it, you won't have much chance of knowing! They very probably also aren't aware of them themselves, so going through this together could be very useful.

Addiction – addiction and ADHD go hand-in-hand. And we aren't just talking drugs and alcohol. Gaming, spending money, gambling, cake, sweets and ice cream to name just a few. The ADHD brain is compulsive and addictive and straight away we have something that can be very heightened with teenagers.

Anger – puberty plus ADHD equals at the very least frustration and at the very worst extreme anger. Some ADHD adolescents are a seething mass of anger from the minute they hit puberty until their early 20s. Boys have it tougher because of their newly acquired testosterone but an ADHD teen without any anger at all is extremely rare indeed.

Attention to Detail – this is an infuriating one for most ADHD people. We think we are concentrating, and we think we are being accurate, but we very often leave words out of sentences, make a spelling mistake when we know very well how to spell the word or write a mobile phone number down missing out a digit. Attention to detail is very difficult when you have a brain that is constantly wanting to move onto the next thing.

Authority – and not liking it! It's a very rare ADHD teen who likes authority. Teenagers especially will kick against parents, grandparents, teachers, referees, Scoutmasters and anybody else who has the audacity to tell them what to do! There is a caveat. If an ADHD teenager respects you, they won't have such a problem with authority. But on the whole anybody in authority has to earn the respect of an ADHD teenager. Their brain naturally wants to rebel against any authority figure.

Boredom – this is a trait that will affect an ADHD person all their life. Their brain naturally craves excitement, adrenaline and something interesting to do. So if you hear your teen wailing, 'I'm bored,' on a very regular basis do not be surprised. It is actually their brain telling them that it is understimulated, but they won't know that, so they will be forever badgering you for something to do because they are SO BORED!

Something to watch out for. Being bored can lead to danger. And by that I mean criminal danger. Boredom can lead to going to the shops and stealing, getting into fights over nothing and being dared by mates to do risky activities. So keeping your teenager occupied and busy with lots of adrenaline-giving activities is much safer than allowing them to become bored on a regular basis.

Buying Things – if you have a teenager who seems to want to buy something every single time you go out or is forever on Amazon or eBay ... this is because the thought of something new will stimulate their brain. New equals exciting.

Bright and Sparkly – one of the ways you can spot an ADHD person is by how much sparkle they are wearing! ADHD brains are drawn to bright, neon and sparkly items. Whether that's clothes, shoes, jewellery or stationery. The brighter and sparklier the better.

Brain Fog – Inattentive ADHD people especially will talk about feeling their brains are constantly surrounded by fog or cotton wool. They find it very hard to clarify their thoughts. For others brain fog can be intermittent. It can mean that we can forget how to spell a word or even what the word is. Our brain can just become foggy or unclear.

Breaking Things – this trait gets a lot worse if you have the coexisting condition of dyspraxia, but ADHD alone can make people clumsy. Often teenagers won't pay attention to what they are doing, will get distracted when they are putting something down like a drink, and before you know it that drink is on the floor and the cup smashed. This trait is way worse for some than others. It's usually caused by a combination of inattention, distraction, impatience and boredom. Because it's not very exciting, making sure a cup gets put back on the worktop, so their brain will have moved on to something far more stimulating, meaning they don't pay attention to what they are doing in the moment.

Compulsivity – a lot of people don't even really know what this means. But an ADHD brain is compulsive. Which means if it starts something – it doesn't want to stop. This particularly relates to food! And with teenagers it can be gaming, watching box sets, shopping and most definitely eating and drinking.

Once the ADHD brain gets a taste for something it likes, it doesn't let go! Meaning anything that is proving exciting to the ADHD brain, your teenager is going to have a very hard time stopping.

Concentration – you probably know struggling to concentrate is a classic ADHD problem. Have some patience with your teenager over this one because sometimes, even when they really do want to concentrate, their brain just isn't interested. At school this can become a major problem, especially if they want to learn, but their brain is finding something else far more interesting. I remember trying to concentrate so many times at school but it was often impossible – usually because the teacher or the subject wasn't stimulating enough. I knew I had to concentrate and get the information in, but my brain just would not engage.

Clown of the Class – this is something ADHD psychiatrists will ask you to look for in your childhood school reports. Were you known as the clown of the class? An ADHD kid who is bored at school will find something to occupy themselves. This is very often making classmates laugh. I remember in my senior school reports, it said 'likes to set herself up as the clown of the class'. I was deeply offended. I WAS the clown of the class and proud of it! Very annoying for the teachers, though, I'm quite sure.

Clumsiness – ADHD teenagers can take clumsiness to a new level. Falling over, tripping up steps, falling off kerbs, bumping into things, dropping things and breaking things can all feature very regularly.

Coexisting conditions – this is a very big subject so it gets a chapter all of its own. But for now let me tell you ADHD psychiatrists say 'ADHD is a big umbrella and a lot comes under it'. By this they mean 80% of people with ADHD have at least one other coexisting condition, for example: dyslexia, dyspraxia, sensory processing disorder, and a whole host of others. An estimated 50% of people with ADHD actually have two or more of these. So we will go into a lot more detail later in the book.

Distraction – ADHD teenagers both get distracted themselves and are masters at distracting others. As soon as they are bored, they will want to attract others' attention to have a laugh with or at the very least talk to. They will get distracted themselves when anything is boring, isn't stimulating enough or their brain gets foggy. You may well see mention of them being distracted or distracting others in their school reports.

Disorganisation – the vast majority of ADHD teenagers struggle hugely with organisation. You might see them living in complete and utter chaos and be itching to organise their room, wardrobe or school bag for them. But I can guarantee if you do, it won't be long before it's just as messy again, which is perplexing and frustrating. Try as hard as they might, it's very easy for ADHD adolescents to become disorganised because they do everything quickly, are constantly buying things so get overwhelmed with too much 'stuff' and putting everything away in its place is just so boring when you have an ADHD brain looking for something a lot more exciting than that!

Difficulty Making Decisions – this applies to some but not all. Personally I've never had any problem making decisions and if anything make them far too quickly with not enough thought. But I've met numerous ADHD clients who say that making a decision is the hardest part of their ADHD. So if you have a teenager who dithers and can't seem to make even the smallest decision, for example, what he wants for his dinner, understand that this can be a real problem for some teenagers, and they will need some help around the process of making a decision.

Drama Queen and Diva – the times I had these comments thrown at me as a teenager! As an adult, I'm quite proud to be a drama queen and a diva, but I wasn't so happy with it at 13. A lot of ADHD teenagers are show-offs. They like to be the centre of attention because it feeds their adrenaline-seeking brain. They are often funny, enjoy making people laugh because it gives them the buzz they crave, but that can soon tip over into being told off for 'always wanting to be the centre of attention', being a drama queen or a diva. These kids need to be shipped into drama clubs and stage schools as soon as possible. It gives them an outlet, adrenaline and potentially a career!

Danger – a lot of ADHD teenagers, particularly boys, but also girls, don't seem to have any fear of danger. They will throw themselves off cliffs into the sea, climb up high trees or four-storey scaffolding without any thought as to what danger they are putting themselves in. This is yet again because it gives them a huge buzz but can at worst be life-threatening so it's definitely something you need to be aware of and talk to your teenager about. They won't know why they do it until you explain it to them.

Debt – and problems managing money. It's a very rare ADHD person indeed who is good at money management and budgeting. The vast majority find all that terribly boring and restricting and are constantly overdrawn, in debt, having County Court Judgments made against them and, as they get older, bailiffs knocking on the door. And that's before you even bring in the ones who have the coexisting condition of dyscalculia, meaning anything to do with numbers is a nightmare.

Emotional Dysregulation – if I could make those two words flash in neon with fireworks coming out of them I would. I cannot begin to tell you how big an issue this is for all ADHD people, but especially teenagers. I hated science and loathed my science teacher, so sadly again you won't get the scientific explanation from me, but I can assure you that emotional dysregulation is a serious problem for most ADHD teens. What it means is the area of our brain that is supposed to regulate emotion doesn't do it properly. This is such a huge issue it gets a whole chapter of its own and it's definitely a red flag for a trait that affects teenagers more than anybody.

Eating Disorders – especially but not exclusively with girls, eating disorders often feature, and yet again, especially in the teenage years. I was a dreadful compulsive eater and binge eater, which only stopped when I was finally diagnosed with ADHD and put on the right medication. So compulsive eating is most definitely one of the disordered eating styles you might see. But also anorexia, bulimia and less so ARFID (avoidant/restrictive food intake disorder).

Ehlers-Danlos Syndrome – this is one of the lesser-known coexisting conditions, but it can be quite a serious issue. EDS is a disorder where the skin and connective tissue – both externally and internally – don't regenerate and heal as they should. Usually the first way to spot it is if your child's scars don't mend well. And instead of healing invisibly they are left with a splayed-out white marking. ADHD teens who are hypermobile need to be checked out for EDS as this is another good indicator.

Entrepreneurial Skills – it's widely accepted that all entrepreneurs have ADHD. And if it's not all of them, it's certainly most of them. Sometimes you will see signs of this even before your children hit adolescence. It's not unusual for 8-year-olds to start selling things to their friends in the playground. But often the first signs of entrepreneurship will show up in teenagers. ADHD teens want things and they aren't interested in waiting for them. So the ones with entrepreneurial tendencies will start up little businesses and ways of earning money in their teens. This is strongly to be encouraged. Because the alternative is where they don't think they need to earn it and they will just take it instead! So if your teen does show signs of entrepreneurship, it's definitely worth encouraging. And with a bit of luck they'll make millions and keep you in the style to which you would like to become accustomed!

FIdgeting – very often the first thing an ADHD child will get into trouble for. Fidgeting and ADHD really do go together. The important thing to know here is that by fidgeting, your teenager is allowing their brain to be stimulated enough for them to be able to concentrate.

So if they have to keep one leg shaking, or their fingers drumming, or they are doodling, know that they are doing this to stimulate their brain enough to focus and concentrate on what they need to. Finding ways for them to fidget that don't drive the rest of the family insane is obviously paramount. I was a doodler as a child. As long as I had a pen and paper, I could doodle and colour-in to my heart's content, and that allowed me to be calm. Fidgeting is a serious problem with ADHD people because if we can't do it, it literally drives us round the twist. And we get very frustrated and irritable. We need to keep something moving to be able to function normally.

Forgetfulness – poor short-term memory is a major problem for most ADHD people. You might think your teenager is being purposefully evasive, not answering questions they should know the answer to, or even that they're lying, when actually they have genuinely forgotten what it is you're expecting them to remember. Usually with ADHD teens long-term memory isn't a problem so they may well be able to remember something they did when they were five but not what they did five minutes ago. I have staggered myself with how forgetful I can be and how poor my short-term memory is, so bear with your teenager who is particularly forgetful. It can be as annoying and frustrating for them as it is for those around them.

Focusing Problems – attempting to focus and hold focus can be very difficult for ADHD teenagers. Their brain can be like Spaghetti Junction with hundreds of thoughts firing-off constantly so focusing on one thing can be extremely difficult. And it's really not as easy as just being told that you need to focus. Often the circumstances have to be exactly right for somebody to focus. I can only focus in complete silence, which is how I'm writing this book. If there's any sort of noise or sound, I lose focus instantly. All teens with ADHD will be different and some actually need noise – background noise, white noise or music – to focus.

Friendship Issues – it's a rare ADHD teenager who doesn't have some problems with friendships. So many ADHD traits feed into this, but to give you an example or two. ADHD brains want everything their own way and they like to feel that they are in charge. So in a friendship group, this can soon become very annoying for the other members. Also ADHD teenagers will say things impulsively and lose good friends because they haven't been able to think before they speak. Being forgetful when it comes to returning texts and responding to invitations can also make us appear uninterested. Getting bored with friends is another ADHD problem. As soon as somebody doesn't stimulate our brain and keep us interested, we will wander off in search of someone more interesting. Having said that, loads of ADHD people do have a lot of good friends. A good chunk of these are probably also ADHD or neurodiverse in some way and almost certainly will have the same shared interests.

Good in a Crisis – you won't see this on many lists of ADHD traits, but it's perfectly true. When an ADHD brain gets flooded with adrenaline, it sees things so much more clearly and calmly than normally. So while neurotypicals might freeze, become flustered and not be able to think straight, you will find the ADHD person as cool as a cucumber because the adrenaline has actually allowed their brain to be still and takes things in more easily than normal. This is why ADHD adults make fantastic paramedics. Remember that when you are helping them consider suitable careers.

Good Sense of Humour – the vast majority of ADHD people have a very good sense of humour. They can see the funny side of everything. And they don't take life too seriously. This can get them into trouble, but it can also make them hugely popular and the life and soul of any party. ADHD teenagers are notorious for getting into trouble for finding things funny that they really shouldn't. Like people falling over. And funerals.

Hypermobility – your 13-year-old might be thrilled that he can bend his thumb back far enough to touch his arm, or twist his legs into some incredible positions. But sadly being hypermobile is actually an indication of EDS.

Hyperactivity – possibly the most famous of all the ADHD traits! The interesting thing is that hyperactivity doesn't have to be physical. So while your teenager may well be flinging themselves all over your house, not able to sit still, needing to be on the go constantly, and never being able to settle to watch a film or a theatre show – there are some ADHD teens who are the polar opposite of this and the hyperactivity can all be in their head. A psychiatrist told me this years ago. When I told him I could be extremely lazy and lie on the sofa for hours, he tapped his forehead and said, 'the hyperactivity can all be in here, my dear. It can all be in here'.

Hyper-Focus – this is when an ADHD brain gets so absorbed by something that everything else becomes insignificant. We can start a project or a task and come so deeply involved that we forget to go to the toilet, forget to eat, forget the world exists outside this particular thing that is stimulating our brain.

Heightened Sense of Justice – this trait is definitely in my top five of the reasons ADHD teenagers get into trouble. We have a very heightened sense of what is right and what is wrong. And what's more we aren't going to shut up about it. Because our brain won't let it go. So if you find your teenager wading into quarrels that are nothing to do with them, don't be surprised. They will be wanting to stick up for what is right and their brain just won't let them turn and walk the other way.

Impatience – an ADHD brain isn't interested in waiting. If it wants something – it wants it NOW. So if you find your teenager impatient about everything from when their dinner is ready to when you are going to buy them new trainers, don't be surprised.

Impulsivity – another ADHD corker and one that really gets ADHD teenagers into trouble. Their brain is impulsive which means they will say and do things without thinking. Medication helps with this hugely, but I can speak from very personal experience when I say impulsivity has catapulted me into all sorts of difficult situations and it's more heightened during the teenage years.

Inattention – another whopper that is going to feature heavily in the teenage years. There are loads of reasons why teenagers don't pay attention. High up on the list is because they are bored, their brain isn't suitably stimulated or something else is distracting their attention. It's also why teenagers can be incredibly clumsy, bumping into doorframes, knocking drinks over and breaking bones. They literally don't pay enough attention to what they are doing so are frequently having mishaps.

Interrupting – If you have a teenager who is constantly interrupting you, however many times you tell them they are doing it, let me explain why this happens. Usually it's because their very poor short-term memory can't hang onto the information they want to share until you finish your (interminably!) long sentence. So their brain and mouth will literally explode with the information before it forgets it. That's the main reason, but it can also be that whatever you are saying is tediously boring and the ADHD teen thinks what they have to say is MUCH more interesting. So they'll crack on with their interesting stuff, shutting you up ASAP! Some ADHD people have the extremely irritating habit of finishing sentences for others. I have friends who do this and I know I'm guilty of it myself!

Internal Motor – I almost cried when I read this was an ADHD trait. I'd never been able to explain to anybody how I felt I just couldn't stop. How I had to keep going however exhausted I was. But now I understand that 'feeling you have an internal motor' is most definitely connected to ADHD. The medication helps with this massively and I would say is one of the most beneficial aspects for me. I no longer feel that I can't stop. I can stop and it's bliss.

Immaturity – doesn't always apply but it can do. They estimate that ADHD children and teenagers can be up to 30% less mature than their actual age. This becomes hugely relevant when your teenager is getting into trouble for not acting like a 15-year-old. You will need to explain to teachers that although your ADHD daughter might be 15, she potentially has the maturity of a 12-year-old.

IBS – irritable bowel syndrome. This is way more common than you think. There are some ADHD teenagers who aren't troubled by IBS at all, but there are a lot who find it debilitating. My very wise counsellor, then counselling supervisor, explained it beautifully – just why IBS and ADHD are connected. 'Simple,' she said. 'The brain works too quickly, hence so does the digestive system.' So before you go for gluten or wheat intolerance testing, whip into a chemist, or even a supermarket, and buy some anti-spasmodic IBS medication and see if this transforms your teenager's tummy and toilet problems. It nearly always does.

Job Hopping – when I was 17 and started work, I could never understand why I spent the first three months of every job full of anxiety that I was going to screw up and get things wrong. Months three to six I was as happy as Larry, but from month six on I started to get bored. Of course I now know this is pure ADHD, but at the time I would leap from one job to the next. I've met many teenagers who only last days in jobs before they are looking for another one. It's because they are always thinking there is something better round the corner – something more exciting, something better paid – and their brain propels them to look for new and more exciting opportunities.

Know-alls – I've met hundreds of ADHD teenagers who think they know everything and I was exactly the same. ADHD teenagers are very sure of themselves and think they know best about just about everything. They will have little patience with teachers who they think are stupid or don't know their subject well enough and even less tolerance when it comes to sports and anything competitive, if they don't have respect for the team captain or the teacher.

Low Self-Esteem – sometimes this will be very obvious and your teen maybe very vocal about how much they hate themselves, how they don't want to have ADHD, how rubbish they are at everything. But sometimes low self-esteem can be silent. It can also be random and inconsistent. So, for example, I've always been confident (some would say arrogant!) about some areas of my life and utterly scathing and full of self-loathing about others.

A heartbreaking but true statistic is by the age of 10, the average ADHD child will have heard 20,000 negative messages. That's averagely five more per day than a neurotypical child. What does that do to your self-esteem? Always worth remembering this.

Lying – this can be mildly worrying or majorly dangerous. ADHD teenagers don't all lie, but the ones who do usually do it to liven up their life, to get more of something like food or money, or to get themselves out of a sticky situation.

Lack of Motivation – this can infuriate parents and many ADHD teenagers are seen as lazy layabouts. More usually what is going on is that their brain is not stimulated enough by whatever it is you want them to do. If that's homework, tidying their room, sorting out their school bag or anything else dull and uninteresting, their lack of motivation will be at its peak. This usually features a lot more with Inattentive ADHD teens than Hyperactive/Impulsive and Combined ADHD ones. But absolutely every ADHD teen lacks motivation when what is being required of them doesn't stimulate their brain.

Losing Things – ADHD teenagers nearly always have a major problem with losing things. This is because their short-term memory doesn't remember where they have put something. Wherever they put their front door keys down, or their school bag or their school shoes or their school tie, that information just isn't interesting enough for their brain to hang onto it, so an hour later when they are looking, they aren't going to have a clue where they have put it.

Lateness – largely because ADHD adolescents are mostly time blind. This means we literally don't have a clue how to work out how long something is going to take. We don't have the foggiest how long ago something was in the past and find it difficult to judge how long things are going to take in the future. This often leads to us being late because we just cannot judge time.

Meltdowns – the official reason for these is that the brain becomes overwhelmed and the teenager cannot regulate their emotions. I know that meltdowns happen usually because a teenager isn't getting their own way! This can be for literally thousands of different reasons. But if things aren't going their way, they aren't getting their fair share, they feel they are being controlled or told what to do, you are likely to have some sort of meltdown on your hands.

Memory Problems – this can be a major problem and really should not be under-estimated. We have a very poor short-term memory although our long-term memory can be quite good. But don't be surprised if your teenager cannot remember what they did an hour ago and they aren't necessarily lying. They might not be able to recall what subjects they had at school today nor what they had for lunch. These things can literally slip out of their mind and be very difficult to recall.

Nothing Ever Being Enough – extremely common with teenagers who want everything and they want it now. They won't want to wait for anything. They will want the latest gadgets, trainers, tracksuits, haircuts and everything else as soon as they come out because they will never be satisfied with what they have. It's their ADHD brain pushing them for something new, exciting and different.

Not Thinking of the Consequences – this is very difficult for non-ADHD people to understand, but I promise you it's absolutely true. An ADHD brain does not have the ability to think of the consequence. It's quite staggering the difference medication makes to this. But if your ADHD teen is not medicated, don't expect them to naturally think of the consequence of anything, because their brain just literally does not do this.

Not Finishing Things – classic ADHD. This is primarily because they get bored and want to do something more exciting. So if your teenager is constantly starting new sports or learning new musical instruments or starting new after-school classes and then giving up – don't be surprised. I was very surprised to find out, in my late 40s, that I had a reputation for not finishing things. When I finished my counselling training a lot of people expressed surprise! I hadn't realised I had a reputation for not finishing things, but apparently I did.

Outspoken – this is the polite way of saying we don't know how to sugar-coat things. ADHD teenagers will say it as it is. They rarely think about taking people's feelings into account or wondering how they will come across. If they think something – they will say it.

Over-sharing – ADHD teenagers aren't very good at gauging how much they should share with classmates, friends, teachers or anybody they come into contact with. They tend to be very open and honest and aren't very good at working out what they should perhaps keep to themselves.

Overthinking – if there were Olympic medals for this, it would be an ADHD person who would win it. ADHD teenagers take overthinking to a new level. Their ADHD brain will ruminate, go over things, won't be able to let things go – and their thinking can get them into a lot of trouble. It can also bring on anxiety, at its worst full-blown obsessive compulsive disorder (OCD) and can destroy friendships and relationships. Overthinking is a real problem for

ADHD people, and it's especially heightened during the teenage years.

Obesity – a problem for some and not for others. As a teenager I wanted to eat everything in sight. I had a mother who controlled what I ate so the minute I went to work at 17 I ate for England. I think I probably put on about five stone in my late teens so do look out for this with your teenagers. It will be their impulsive and compulsive brain that could lead to obesity problems.

Overly Compassionate – you might not think this would be much of a problem, but if I tell you it's seen me thrown out of the prison service three times because I've been 'overly compassionate'[1] to ADHD boys behind bars, you will see that it can be a real problem.

Our compassion can be for different things. Mine has always been for marginalised members of society like the homeless and ex-offenders. But your teenager might be very compassionate when it comes to animals or refugees or anything that pricks their conscience. You need to keep an eye on it because being overly compassionate can get them into trouble. I've actually known teenagers get arrested because their extreme compassion has led to criminal activities.

Overwhelm – this is not talked about much but it needs to be, because it massively affects behaviour. ADHD brains are peculiar in that they can go from 'Everything is absolutely fine and I'm very happy, thank you very much' to 'This is all too much and I just can't cope' in a split second.

Overwhelm with teenagers is very often school based. They could become overwhelmed with the amount of homework they have to do. Or overwhelmed with the amount of different subjects they are expected to study. Or overwhelmed when they leave the structure of school and go to university. Suddenly it's all too much and they can't cope.

Take it from me, feelings of ADHD overwhelm are absolutely awful. It can lead to severe depression and feelings of hopelessness and

---

[1] Overly compassionate or as I call it – caring!

uselessness. So if you hear your ADHD teen say they are feeling overwhelmed or more likely 'they can't do this anymore' take it very seriously and do something to lessen their load. They might not even know why they are overwhelmed or that they have taken on too much, but you can help them identify what the problem is and reduce the pressure.

Pushing **Boundaries** – another massive red flag when it comes to keeping your teen safe and on the right side of the law. Their brain naturally wants to push boundaries. Because staying within boundaries is boring and we so HATE boring! So look at ways your teen can push themselves in a legal and positive way. Often this is through sport or drama/singing/dance and performance of any kind. Much better that they are pushing boundaries to become team captain of the school football team or pushing to get out of the chorus and into a lead role at their drama club than pushing boundaries with the law.

Procrastination – or putting things off. I've never had much of a problem with this one because of that wretched internal motor, but I know hundreds of ADHD people who struggle hugely with procrastination. With teenagers, this is going to be putting off anything that's boring. So you can guarantee tidying rooms, doing homework, having baths and showers, cleaning teeth, cleaning their shoes before school is going to be put off for as long as they possibly can. It's quite literally the fact that their brain is not stimulated enough by that activity.

You can usually get over this by offering them some sort of reward after the boring activity. Doesn't have to be monetary. It might just be sitting in the front seat of the car on the way to school, but something needs to motivate them to get over their procrastination.

Perfectionism – and things having to be just right. This is often mistaken for OCD, but there is a big difference. Perfectionism does not have negative thoughts attached, so while your child might have a complete meltdown if they spill ink on their brand-new notepad, there won't be any negative thoughts attached to that. Perfectionism is tough. I'm actually diagnosed with it. And it's crippling.

Because when things aren't perfect, we can't function. So it's not something to be taken lightly.

People Pleasing – in my experience this relates much more to girls than boys, but that's not to say boys don't have it. People pleasing comes from low self-esteem and not valuing yourself enough. A lot of ADHD teenagers will become people pleasers because they realise that they are different, and they don't necessarily fit in with a lot of other people so to make themselves more attractive to friendship groups for example, they will people please in an attempt to be accepted.

Promiscuity – this can actually be linked with people pleasing. I've met many girl teenagers who bitterly regret earlier teenage promiscuity which they now realise came from having low self-esteem. A very long time ago I met a 20-something who told me they 'had slept with half of High Wycombe' in an attempt to be accepted. So do look out for promiscuity in your teenager as it's a big indicator of low self-esteem and wanting to be liked and accepted.

Queueing – even the word makes me shudder. It's a very rare ADHD teenager who can queue without getting irritated at the least, steaming angry at the most. Queueing really is our worst nightmare. Not only is it boring, but there is very little we can do to stimulate our brains, unless we have a smartphone handy of course. But even that loses its appeal after twenty minutes of no movement. It's no coincidence that Access cards get used most at theme parks and anywhere an ADHD person is expected to queue.

Quickness – not all, but most ADHD people like to do things quickly. That includes speaking, eating, writing, driving, and anything else where there is a choice of speed. Mostly, it's their brain wanting to push on with the next more interesting thing and also to avoid our arch nemesis – boredom. Speed is also a great adrenaline giver.

Rejection **Sensitive Dysphoria** – this is a relatively new term but something that needs to be taken extremely seriously. ADHD teenagers do not like rejection. Not only rejection but also humiliation, which they take as rejection. They can also perceive rejection when it's not really there. So watch out for this because it will be heightened during puberty. Anything that they can perceive as rejection, they will. And not only that but it will hurt. Really hurt.

Ruminating – not to be confused with overthinking. Ruminating is when an ADHD brain gets stuck on one subject and cannot move on from it. This is another one where we would win the Oscar if there was one for it. We can ruminate over something for a very long time and with teenagers, this can get them into trouble. I've worked with teenagers where ruminating and 'not being able to let something go' has caused them to get into all sorts of serious trouble.

Risk-Taking – some ADHD kids have so much anxiety that they aren't great risk-takers. Some on the other hand take this to the extreme. Anything that will give them an adrenaline shot or a buzz, they will catapult themselves into without taking the consequences into account. Risk-taking can be anything from taking money out of Mum's purse to flinging themselves off a cliff into the sea not knowing what is beneath. It's a serious trait and one that causes a myriad of problems.

Sleep Problems – it was only in very recent years that they decided sleep problems were no longer a comorbidity of ADHD. No longer a comorbidity because actually they are part of the condition. Sleep problems present in numerous ways with ADHD teenagers. A lot of them have trouble falling asleep and it can literally take hours for them to switch their brain off. Others wake up in the night because their brain is so active it wakes them up. And a lot wake up far too early and can't get back to sleep again because they can't switch their brain off. Sleep-talking and sleep-walking are also common due to the over-active brain.

Speed – most ADHD teenagers want to do everything at great speed. They haven't patience or time for slow walkers, slow teachers, slow football captains or anybody else who is going to hold them back.

A lot of them talk extremely quickly, some so quickly you can't actually hear all their words, and they like to do everything at great speed so they can move onto the next exciting thing.

Thinking **We Know Best** – I did have a snigger to myself when I first read this was an actual ADHD trait. I had spent fifty years thinking I knew best and knowing that it couldn't possibly be true but still strongly feeling it! Then I find out it's part of this condition. Our brain literally thinks it knows best about everything. This can be useful if you are a captain of industry, a sports captain or a politician, but can also get you into all sorts of trouble, especially with friends, work colleagues and in relationships.

Thrill-Seeking – very similar to its twin, risk-taking. You will find most ADHD teenagers are hellbent on finding thrills. For some, this comes with a daily delivery from Amazon, and for others from extreme sports, like snowboarding and bungee jumping.

Time-Blindness – this is a fascinating one. Something about the ADHD brain means we are very poor judges of how long ago something was, how long something is going to take to do in the present and just how long something might be in the future. This is worse for some than others, but means that mostly ADHD people have a reputation for being late!

Talking a Lot – or the less pretty version – verbal diarrhoea. There are some ADHD kids who stimulate their brains by talking. Or as my mother used to call it 'liking the sound of my own voice'. I have known parents who have literally been driven round the twist by an ADHD teenager who just does not seem able to shut up. I promise you it's because they are stimulating their brain by talking and medication truly helps!

Unable **to Relax or Chill** – this goes back to that horrible internal motor we were talking about earlier. An ADHD teenager may find it absolutely impossible to sit on the sofa and watch a film for two hours. They won't be able to relax and just do nothing. They will constantly need something to fiddle with or a phone to be on or a second activity to keep their brain stimulated.

Understanding Instructions and Directions – this is a very little-known trait of ADHD, but one that causes massive problems at school and in any educational setting. Sometimes an ADHD brain just does not understand what it is being told to do. And the best way to resolve this is by looking at how somebody else is doing it.

So for example, at a ballet class, what the ballet teacher is explaining might mean nothing to your daughter, but the minute she sees somebody else doing a new step, she will be able to copy it.

Very Sensitive – something I used to get thrown at me a lot as a teenager. ADHD teenagers can really take things to heart. They are often emotional and do take things exceptionally personally. So rather than accusing them of being a drama queen, or a diva, accept that they are more emotional than neurotypical teenagers and, yes, they are very sensitive. But that doesn't mean they are *over*-sensitive.

Wanting to Win – one of my all-time favourite teenage clients told me that 'coming second was in effect losing'. I totally agree with him. ADHD people, especially teenagers, like to win at everything. Coming second is therefore losing and we don't like it.

Wanting Everything Our Own Way – another delightful trait that doesn't win us many friends. Because we think we know best, we do tend to want things our own way. We don't like giving up that power to other people and would much rather everything was done in the way we think best. Particularly a strong trait for ADHD teenagers.

Zoning Out – this is when ADHD teens get called daydreamers, or told off in school for not concentrating or not focusing. Zoning out is something an ADHD brain will do when it is not being stimulated enough. Or when something has become boring because they've been doing it for too long. Some people, particularly Inattentive ADHD brains, zone out a lot more than others but for most it is purely when things get too boring or under stimulating for them that they will zone out and go somewhere far more fun in their head.

So now you know most of the traits affecting your ADHD teenager we can delve a lot deeper into what is going on in their brain and how you can best manage them to ensure the fabulous future they deserve.

11
HAVE YOU HAD ALL THEIR COEXISTING CONDITIONS DIAGNOSED?

I can't begin to tell you how important this is so please don't go thinking 'well we've got the ADHD diagnosis sorted. That took ruddy years and now we are good to go'. That's almost always not the case.

The ADHD gods aka psychiatrists decided a long time ago that 80% of people with ADHD have one coexisting condition. And a whopping 50% have two or more.

I'm a pretty good example. I thought, aged 51, my Combined, moderate-to-severe ADHD diagnosis totally made sense of my life. I was thankful to at last understand myself.

But then I carried on counselling lots of adolescent and adult ADHD clients and as they started talking about some of their coexisting conditions, I thought 'but I do all that, and more' in some cases. I distinctly remember a terribly nice middle class lady telling me all about her dyspraxia and thinking 'Blimey, if she's diagnosed with this, maybe I've got it'.

Six months later I was the proud but shocked owner of my own dyspraxia diagnosis. But mine came with gold knobs on. 'Severe dyspraxia with 1% processing and 1% motor skills!' Good grief. I'd known I was clumsy but 1%?!

So much MORE now made sense. Why I could never understand how anything worked. Why I could only open my (daily) Amazon deliveries by stabbing the box with a knife – no clue how to unpack or open it. And why I could never follow a James Bond film or any TV show that had flashbacks or intricate plots.

Then I was diagnosed with sensory processing disorder (tons of ADHD people have this) which explained why I only wear denim and cotton and can't eat nuts because they taste like wood.

Then my third coexisting condition! The real villain of the piece: dyscalculia. The 'numbers version of dyslexia' and the reason I had failed my 12-plus 'so spectacularly' when everyone and his dog had thought I'd pass and get into the grammar school.

Now I did finally have all the pieces of my jigsaw. And my whole life did make sense.

So please, PLEASE don't think ADHD explains everything. So rarely is that the case. And in my firm opinion, it's the coexisting conditions that can screw up your life more than the actual ADHD.

It did mine. I spent four years at a low-achieving secondary modern school, bored rigid, where babies and boyfriends were what most of my peers seemed to want. Three of the fifth-years in my form room were heavily pregnant when I joined! Whereas I craved learning and was held back by teachers who weren't even qualified to teach me to O level, resulting in a dismal drama CSE grade 1 in my best subject.

So let's take a whistle-stop but no less important tour through the most likely coexisting conditions and what to look out for.

Dyslexia – A very common one. And dangerous too. Because once diagnosed with dyslexia, all your teen's troubles will be put down to their dyslexia diagnosis. I personally have yet to meet one person diagnosed with dyslexia who doesn't actually have ADHD (including you, Matt Hancock). Dyslexia is the one teachers do spot and does get picked up in schools. These kids will have problems with English and writing right from the start. They will probably struggle with spelling, punctuation, sentence construction, comprehension and 'letters jumping all over the page'. So it's not hard for teachers to pick this one up – but 99% of them, if not 100%, won't have thought this might be linked to undiagnosed ADHD. So it's up to you to dig deeper to find out if there is more going on.

Then its numbers' sister:

Dyscalculia. These kids get picked up far less frequently. They might be good at elements of maths – I was a whizz with fractions and algebra. But give me a column of figures to add up five times? I'd give you five different answers every time. Dyscalculia can mean kids struggle with analogue clocks and watches, get 'quarter to' and 'quarter past' mixed up (hence I would only see clients at something o'clock!) and struggle to remember routines in PE or dance classes.

Dyspraxia or DCD (developmental coordination disorder) is also very common. Dyspraxia can mean so much more than being clumsy. If your teen seems to be covered in bruises or breaking bones more than their mates, have a google of dyspraxia. We can bump into door frames and furniture, fall off kerbs, drop food down us every time we eat and have real problems with motor skills like riding bikes. The first time I stood on a Segway I was off it within 30 seconds. It terrified me. I had no ability to balance whatsoever. We also tend to press very hard when we write. I broke more pen nibs at school than I care to remember. And my writing could always be seen three pages below!

And the final of the big 4 D's:

Dysgraphia. This is a far more complex condition and can prove hugely debilitating to those with it, especially if it's not diagnosed. It's well worth researching if you think your teen's writing issues go beyond dyslexia. Dysgraphia often means adolescents will struggle to hold a pen, write in a straight line, form letters back to front or have all the information in their head but not be able to get that information down in any coherent form.

If your child has reached their teens without one or several of these being picked up, it's massively important they are screened for them now. It's not too late. And please don't assume school would have picked it up if it was there. I've worked with a 29- and a 44-year-old both with severe but undiagnosed dysgraphia. Teachers aren't as yet trained to pick up ADHD, let alone any of these coexisting conditions.

IBS or irritable bowel syndrome – 'tummy trouble' goes down better than discussing toilet habits with teens. Or anyone for that matter! I've lost count of the number of clients having their kids tested for wheat or lactose intolerance, colitis and Crohn's disease when all along it's been IBS. If your teen starts complaining of constipation or the opposite – going to the loo six times a day – or crippling tummy pains, whip to the supermarket and pick up some antispasmodic tablets – in the UK Buscopan are a safe bet. These won't do them any harm if the problem isn't IBS but will be a blessed relief if it is.

Alexithymia – thankfully, this is a very rare trait, but for those with it, and especially their partners, it brings a lot of problems especially with relationships. In simple terms, people with alexithymia don't feel emotions. They struggle to feel and definitely to express how they are feeling. Having family members with this condition I know how crippling it can be. They just don't understand how to feel love or express it and I've seen the isolation and feelings of rejection it can bring to the people who love them. For the person with alexithymia they may or may not realise they have the condition. Some think the way they feel is perfectly normal. Others know that they should be able to feel emotions but just aren't able to.

Fibromyalgia and Chronic Fatigue. The very earliest I've seen either of these come on is early teenage years. Far more common is later in life, from 30–40 years of age onwards. Both of them can be seriously debilitating and fibromyalgia brings with it a lot of joint and muscle pain as well as the utter exhaustion. If you have a teenager who seems to be extremely lethargic, never has any energy and is always complaining they are wiped out or constantly knackered – it's well worth looking into both of these because they can be coexisting conditions alongside ADHD.

There are a surprising amount of coexisting conditions that go alongside ADHD, even more than I have given you above, but the good news is I have yet to meet one person with all of them. I've met several people with a handful of them though and it's very important you get these diagnosed. Very, very, VERY important. And the reason for that is that if a child gets to their teens without any of these conditions being diagnosed, it can massively negatively impact their education and also cripple their self-esteem.

For example, if they are struggling with dysgraphia but nobody has identified it, to avoid feeling humiliated they will instead skip classes, potentially avoid school altogether, or distract their friends and become the clown of the class in an attempt to cover up what they see as their failings.

By not identifying coexisting conditions, you are risking your child suffering with depression, anxiety, feelings of low self-worth and 'not being good enough'.

I've worked with clients exactly like this. One example was a boy who had been diagnosed with ADHD and autistic spectrum disorder (ASD) traits. By the time I met him he was 15 and nobody had picked up his dyscalculia, dyspraxia nor his dysgraphia. He had spent years feeling like a complete and utter loser who couldn't do anything like everybody else. To make matters worse – he had spent five years in a very expensive private school, supposedly specialising in children with additional needs! Yet nobody had picked any of this up until he and I worked it out together.

This is why I'm currently on my knees, begging you to make sure your teenager has been assessed for any condition you think might be impacting them.

We can't blame the schools for not picking up these conditions because teachers are not trained in them. Yet. This is something we are desperately trying to get changed. We aren't trying to transform teachers into paediatricians or occupational therapists. But the simple matter is these conditions are going to show up at school more than in any other environment. So if teachers are made more aware of what they are, they can at least flag it up to the parents for them to investigate further.

But at the moment, that is not happening. So please do keep the lines of communication open with your teenager. Get them to be absolutely honest with you about what they are struggling with.

Keep an eye on their grades and if they are doing fantastically well with anything numerical and abysmally in subjects where they have to write words, or vice versa, then dig deeper to find out where those struggles originate from.

One thing I can guarantee is your teenager will not be aware of these conditions and why they might be struggling. I certainly wasn't. I just knew English was a breeze and maths was bloody hard work. If I could go back now and somebody had sat down and asked me what I could do well, and what I struggled with, it wouldn't have been a very long conversation to work out that I have dyscalculia. But nobody was faintly interested. My school just thought I should do better at maths and concentrate harder. My mother wasn't terribly interested because I was doing so well in other subjects so I went undiagnosed until my mid 50s.

I'm absolutely passionate about kids and teenagers being aware of all the conditions they are dealing with. Only then can they get the support they need and only then can we drag their self-esteem off the floor, knowing that their struggles aren't just because they are thick.

12
EMOTIONAL DYSREGULATION – AND ITS MAJOR IMPACT ON YOUR TEENAGER

Now here is one of the first big facts that you need to stamp onto the front of your brain and remember before you react to anything your child does from the age of about 9 to 19!

To give you some idea of how massive this ADHD trait is. It wasn't many years before I wrote this book, that again, the gods of the ADHD world, masquerading as ADHD psychiatrists, decided that they had been wrong all along. For decades they had thought the major impact of ADHD was hyperactivity, inattention, distraction and impulsivity. They had been wrong apparently. Of course, these do feature on a very regular basis for most ADHD teens and adults, but actually the biggest impact on an ADHD person is, drum roll ... emotional dysregulation.

And if you ask anybody with ADHD, whether they believe this to be true, they will nod so violently they will be at risk of dislocating their neck. Everybody with the condition knows all about dysregulated emotions. Neurotypicals without it won't have any clue how this can have such a major impact in every area of an ADHD person's life. So they are going to have to trust me. It does.

I'm always very upfront about the fact that I'm not scientific. In fact, I am probably one of the least scientific people on the planet. I blame my science teacher. She was an utter cow. After two years of her dreary nonsense, aged 12 to 14, I literally flung myself on the form that said I could give up science and concentrate on subjects I enjoyed. So I do apologise, but you are never going to get very scientific explanations from me.

But what you will get is thoughts, feelings and emotions because all of those I understand extremely well, thanks to five-and-a-half years of counselling training. So let me tell you what it feels like to have emotional dysregulation. Particularly in your teens.

Pre-teen years, I had been quite an easy-going, chubby, clumsy tomboy kid. Idolising my father, refusing to wear skirts, happy in my shorts and plimsolls. I spent my life in my sandpit and riding my bike. Nothing troubled me too much, but when puberty hit – it was like a tidal wave. And for me it hit round about the age of 11 or 12. For the non-squeamish amongst you, I think I conveniently started my periods in the summer holidays between junior school and senior school.

I have known of kids hitting puberty at 9. That's the earliest I've heard of but that's not to say it doesn't happen before for some. And there are of course 'late bloomers' who don't get close to puberty till 13 or 14 or even later. But whenever it starts, if that child is ADHD, prepare to take cover. Because everything you've known before is about to change!

I do know the reason for this – just without the scientific terminology. The area of the brain that regulates emotion does not work as it should in an ADHD brain. Put very simply, this means that an ADHD brain does not automatically produce the usual or expected emotional response to situations.

A teenage client of mine summed this up beautifully when he said, 'Oh, does that explain why I cried when my dog died and not my Nan? And I did like my Nan.' He was bang on right.

Sometimes the expected emotions just don't present themselves when you are ADHD. You've heard of teenagers laughing when they are led from a court down to the cells having received a 15-year prison sentence? I can almost guarantee they are ADHD.

Another very unnerving way dysregulated emotion can play out is in your mood. I distinctly remember as a teenager – and only as a teenager, this hasn't happened since – sitting feeling perfectly happy when suddenly a wave of low mood would flood over me. I would sit there perplexed, thinking, 'Oh no, what has happened? Why do I feel like this? What on earth has happened to make me so sad?'.

This could last for anything from twenty minutes to a couple of hours. Then not very long afterwards I would find myself feeling extremely happy – again for no reason. And yet again I would sit there thinking, 'What's happened? What have I been told or what just happened that has made me happy?' and I could never put my finger on anything.

Now of course I know this was dysregulated emotions, but at the time it was extremely perplexing. And worrying. Because each time you feel very sad you think something has happened and you have forgotten what it was. Was somebody being horrible to me? Had somebody said something or done something nasty to me? I couldn't remember, but I knew I felt as miserable as sin. I didn't cross question myself quite so much when I was feeling euphorically happy but I do know it happened for no reason. Sudden feelings of extreme happiness, that everything was right with the world, and I felt wonderful. Now I know this is all absolutely classic emotional dysregulation.

When we are talking emotions of course, we aren't just talking happy or sad. There are hundreds of emotions that can emanate from your adolescent and two I remember feeling very strongly throughout my teens were frustration and irritation. Just about everything frustrated me or irritated me. Just a few random examples from literally thousands, people who talked too slowly, people who walked too slowly, people who disagreed with me, people who told me what to do, people who thought they knew better than me, people who belittled me, or put me down, anything that I didn't feel was just or fair, my two younger brothers who, of course were hugely irritating just for existing, and pretty much everything else about my daily life at home and at school.

So sadly, I can't sit here and tell you which emotions your own teenager is going to produce; that's going to be a (lovely!) surprise for you, but you are going to find their emotions are up and down, sometimes numerous times in one day and although it might be difficult to believe, it's something you need to get your head round very quickly because it is almost definitely going to happen!

So though it might be tempting to say, 'Why have you got that thunderous face on you? You were laughing your head off with your brother twenty minutes ago,' if you don't want a reaction, then keep comments like that unsaid.

Dysregulated emotions are also the reason a lot of teenage girls in particular get called 'drama queen', 'overly sensitive', 'diva' and accused of 'wanting to be the centre of attention'.

And then of course there's anger. Some adolescents are literally angry for 10 years. If you ask them where the anger is coming from, they don't even know. It's just the way they feel. And that anger can sometimes turn to violence. It might be mild, as in kicking the furniture, but it could also go to the quite extreme.

I don't want to scare you, but I am not going to hold back when it comes to telling the truth in this book because that's no use to anybody. Sometimes ADHD teens do get angry and violent and their emotions are so powerful that they will go out and punch the neighbour if their dog is barking too loudly. And as for younger brothers. I've known many who have received a thumping or a punching from an older ADHD teen sibling. I've even known parents who have been black and blue after being pushed and thumped by an angry teen.

Let's take a moment to sympathise with these parents. I've met dozens of them. Some become absolutely terrified of their own children. They still love them of course and want the best for them, but they are scared stiff of where the anger and violence will take them. I've had numerous parents tell me that of course they love their ADHD child, but they really don't like them very much at the moment! They're always very embarrassed about this and worried they will have social services on their doorstep for merely mentioning the fact that their teenager has become a violent bully.

Therapy is a very good place to start. Both for the teenager who will need to vent and have somebody who understands their brain, but also for the parent who could probably do with a bit of empathy and advice from a counsellor who has had an ADHD teenager of their own.

Speaking to an ADHD-experienced therapist about what you are dealing with can be so reassuring and helpful. Parents learn that this is nothing unusual. Being terrified of your own ADHD teenager's moods and anger is perfectly normal and there is a ton of support around for parents going through this. ADHD parenting therapy is one of the most busy areas of my ADHD therapy company.

It's very, VERY difficult to control your emotions when you're an ADHD teenager, so this is where your understanding and compassion for what they are going through needs to be at its peak.

If something is really winding your teenager up – like the next-door neighbour's incessantly barking dog, nip out and have a word with the neighbour yourself before your son explodes. They really do struggle to control their emotions and being laughed at or having the mickey taken out of them, which in their view is humiliating, is the very last thing you want to do. That guarantees you an explosion.

We have to get serious for a minute here as well, because with ADHD there is a higher risk of self-harm and suicide. I would love to be able to say this hasn't touched my life, but in the last year one of my precious young offenders took his own life, due to his dysregulated emotion and the prison service refusing to put him on the correct ADHD medication, which would have regulated them for him.

If your child is self-harming, then there is a lot of very good advice out there and there are also teen ADHD specialist therapists who I strongly recommend you consult if you find out your child is self-harming in any way.

Just remember that while you might not understand how your teenager's emotions can be so up and down, neither can they. They don't have any control over them.

Medication usually evens out emotions, but they are still going to be heightened during puberty.

Just a bit more on puberty …

I really cannot stress enough how your ADHD teenager is going to be affected by puberty. The average age for girls to hit puberty is 11. And for boys – between 8 and 12. The latest either start is usually around the age of 14.

Those of you past this point with children who are already starting to get into trouble might like to cast your mind back to how they were around the age of about 9.

Whenever I've been working with clients and we've worked back to when things started to get rocky, it's nearly always around the age of 9.

ADHD is a condition so massively connected to hormones.

Very simply, an ADHD brain does not have enough dopamine and dopamine is the happy hormone. So until we are diagnosed and medicated, we spend our entire lives seeking that dopamine or happiness injection.

While for all teenagers puberty means different hormones jangling around their bodies, if you times that by about 10, you'll understand how dysregulated an ADHD teen going through puberty feels.

ADHD traits will always be heightened in both girls and boys at the beginning and end of puberty. So as an incredibly rough guide from around 10 to 14, and again from 16 to 19. I'll never forget one mothers face when I told her this. She looked at me with teary eyes and said, 'oh thank God – there's a couple of years' respite in between then?'.

There's good news for the boys here though. Boys puberty starts and ends over very roughly a 7–10-year period and the END of puberty for boys can be more problem-strewn than the beginning, largely because of the testosterone that is now settled nicely in their bodies, bringing with it a whole host of different strong feelings and emotions. Anger being just one example. But. That's it. Done. That's the last time their hormones will be as pronounced and give them anywhere near as much trouble as they will girls.

For ADHD girls, we don't have such good news. The ADHD traits will be heightened every month once they start their menstrual cycle, then again during any pregnancies and yet again during menopause. It is no coincidence that many women are diagnosed in their late 40s and early 50s, when they have started perimenopause and actual menopause. I was 51, so a classic case of menopause-diagnosed ADHD.

If that seems incredibly unfair (and I think it does!) we can balance it out with the fact that boys with ADHD, generalising terribly, tend to struggle with the traits being heightened more for most of their life. This boils down to the fact that girls manage their emotions more easily than boys. But that's meagre compensation when every single month for about thirty years girls can have seriously up-and-down emotions for a good couple of weeks.

Something else to note, if you have a teen who is pregnant, you might suddenly find they are more balanced, regulated and happier than ever before. This is because, for some – not all, but for some ADHD people – when they're pregnant, they feel more calm and relaxed than they ever have before. I've had some mum clients tell me it's almost worth getting pregnant again for the peace of mind, clear head and calmness it brings them.

Probably not something you will be wanting to encourage in your teenager at this point though!

Top Take-Aways

Remember, your teen has as little control over their emotions as you have over yours, and it is puberty making them so erratic. Have some sympathy for them rather than trying to force them to have consistent moods.

Don't Bother ...

Expecting them to behave like their non-ADHD siblings. Or to be as consistent as they were when they were eight. All hell is breaking loose in their body and they WILL come out the other end. Simply accept their changeable moods are not their choice.

DAMAGE LIMITATION TARGETS:

13
MORE COMPASSION AND EMPATHY

You may well have just spat your tea out if your teenager is showing zero compassion towards anything, and seemingly has no empathy whatsoever.

But trust me on this one. ADHD people, and that includes the stroppiest of teenagers, have more compassion and care more deeply than people without ADHD.

It's a very strange one this, and even in the most severe cases where I've had an angry, tortured, raging and hating-the-world teenager sitting in front of me, there has always, always been something that has brought out their compassionate side.

One of my favourite teenagers of all time (and I did love them all so this is high praise!) was particularly pissed off throughout his puberty. Everything drove him insane, from his mother to his sisters to his school. He despised all his classmates and was a raging ball of hatred and anger when I first met him.

But, when he had finished punching walls and thumping his father, at weekends he would volunteer at the local dementia home. And he loved the old ladies as much as they loved him.

His mother could never make sense of this. How could he be so angry, vile and vicious 98% of the time and then turn into such an angel in front of these 90-year-olds?

I got it. Because I was exactly the same. I could never actually work this out in myself when I was young. Everything in the world seemed to make me angry, but I distinctly remember going on holiday to Dorset when I was about 12 and there being a little boy with Down's syndrome. I didn't leave him alone for the whole week. I cared so hugely about this boy, looking after him, playing with him, desperate to never leave him out of anything we were doing, yet it seemed so out of kilter with the rest of my personality at the time. I was nicer to him than I was to anybody in my family!

Now of course, it makes sense. And the good news is – you can actually use this to your advantage when it comes to handling your ADHD adolescent. Something will bring out that compassionate side. Finding it, though, can be the initial problem. But it will be there, even if it is well hidden under numerous layers of 'I hate everyone and everything'.

I have yet to meet an ADHD teenager who isn't passionate about something. The range of those 'somethings' would surprise you. For a lot, it's animals. Every kind of animal. I've had teenagers who have been livid about the way cattle are treated and start joining charities and banging off complaint letters to MPs. Others who are dog-crazy and enraged at people using dogs for fighting. I've met many who feel huge amounts of compassion for homeless people and get very frustrated because if they are under 18 it's unlikely they will be allowed to volunteer at homeless hostels.

We have found ways to make this work. As can you. For example, one client was particularly good at cake-baking so she would make up boxes of iced cupcakes and her mother would deliver them on an ad-hoc 'when her daughter was in the mood' basis to a homeless charity.

As they get older, it will become more obvious where their compassion lies. From my late teens I used to go to London a lot, as I was theatre mad and spent most of my life in Shaftesbury Avenue seeing all the top theatre shows. Every time it broke my heart seeing so many homeless people on the streets. It literally hurt. Physically. I couldn't walk past one without thrusting a £20 note into their hands but it never felt enough and it almost felt dismissive. 'Here you go. Here's twenty quid that will sort your life out. I'm off home.'

It just wasn't enough, I wanted to do more to help, so that compassionate gene found me being part of the very first ever *Big Issue* magazine mentoring scheme for homeless people and there began thirty compassion-filled years of working with the homeless and subsequently ex-offenders. Every minute of which I have absolutely adored. Because it fulfilled that need in me to show compassion to people.

Your ADHD teenager will be exactly the same, so finding what really affects or makes an impact on them is your goal. Television is a very good way of finding this out. Listen out for their comments when they are watching certain programmes. Is it animals or people that inflame their heightened sense of justice, and bring out all that hidden compassion? Items on the news? That's another very good way of finding out what your teenager thinks isn't acceptable and they might want to do something about.

It's important you find out what your teenager is passionate about because this will raise their self-esteem hugely. By doing something good for either people or animals they are going to feel so much better about themselves. They might not be getting much praise or thanks at school, but if they can do something outside of school, because it's something they care deeply about, it really can do wonders for their self-esteem.

Top Take-Aways

Your ADHD teenager will have compassion. However deeply it is buried I promise you, it's there. This has the potential to give them a healthy interest, make them feel good about themselves and raise their wavering self-esteem. Who knows, it might even lead to a career.

Don't Bother …

Looking for this when they are little. It doesn't usually kick in until their early teens onwards.

Don't try to force your own thoughts or feelings on them. This has to come from within themselves.

DAMAGE LIMITATION TARGETS:

14
REJECTION SENSITIVE DYSPHORIA – THE ONE THING EVERY ADHD TEEN HAS BUT DOESN'T WANT

If you've not heard of this before, it's well worth a google. When I was researching online, the first night I had been made aware I might have ADHD, it was when I read about 'Rejection Sensitive Dysphoria' I absolutely KNEW I had ADHD. I'd never before been able to explain my intense feelings of rejection and inability to take jokes aimed at me, nor why it had hurt SO MUCH.

Nobody understands RSD, as it's known, like somebody with ADHD. Although I now learn that it's not completely exclusive to ADHD, it still features in every single ADHD person I have ever met. And I firmly believe, in its severest form, it is connected to ADHD alone. Not that we want it - we would happily give it away, but sadly we don't have that choice.

RSD quite simply means that ADHD people cannot take rejection. It also means they can perceive rejection when it is not really there.

It's a very skewed way of perceiving and feeling both rejection and humiliation.

For some people, this is mild and they only feel it in extreme circumstances. For others, it pervades every area of their life and can be crippling for them. Even life-threatening for some.

There are celebrities, I shall be discreet and not name, who I'm certain have taken their own lives because of RSD. They just could not handle the extreme feelings of rejection when they had become involved in something which was made public and therefore unbearably humiliating.

RSD is painful. Physically painful. I always describe it as 'like little daggers, stabbing you in the stomach.' Rejection can hurt and *perceived* rejection can hurt just as much. Yet again, if there was an Oscar or an Olympic gold medal for feeling rejected when there was no need to, it would be an ADHD person winning it.

One thing to be careful of is the tone of your voice. An ADHD teen can feel rejected if somebody is snappy, sharp, or heaven forbid, sarcastic towards them. This will really hurt. And if they feel hurt they may well react. And by that I mean verbally, by kicking off or having a meltdown.

If teachers or tutors comment to you that your child isn't engaging in classroom discussions, is reticent about putting their hand up in class and 'really should make an effort to participate more' in debates and group activities, do tell them that RSD could be behind the teen's reticence. The fear of getting it wrong, being humiliated and looking like an idiot could well be what is holding them back. RSD is responsible for lack of confidence because the humiliation is literally unbearable.

RSD can feature within your teenager's friendships. If they are in a friendship group and get excluded, for any reason, they will feel massive rejection.

First relationships and crushes are likely to bring on RSD. If a new love interest isn't texting back at the speed the ADHD teenager deems appropriate, RSD will kick in immediately. Even as a grown adult in my 30s and 40s, I've been like this at the start of new relationships. That sickening feeling in your stomach waiting for a text, and then as soon as you've had it, and replied, the sickening feeling comes back, waiting for the next one.

I even know adults with ADHD who won't have relationships at all because the feelings of RSD at the beginning are so intense, they are absolutely unbearably painful. And I get that. It was exactly the same for me.

So expect your teenager's dysregulated emotions to be impacted by feelings of rejection, whether the rejection is there or not. The critical thing to remember here is perceived rejection can hurt just as much as actual.

The best way to help your teenager with this is to sit down and have a good old chat with them about exactly what RSD is and how it might affect them. The more they know about it, the more they will be aware when it's actually happening to them. This won't completely stop the feelings of rejection or humiliation, but it goes a long way to helping them not be destroyed by it.

And make sure other family members understand how rejection and humiliation can be taken and perceived by the ADHD teenager.

Top Take-Aways

Try to avoid saying or doing anything that could possibly be perceived as rejection or humiliation to your ADHD teenager. Know that during their teens, they are going to react more strongly to rejection and humiliation than at any other time in their life.

Make sure they are educated about RSD and remind them that these feelings will always pass, however painful they are at the time.

Don't Bother ...

Telling them to snap out of it or that they are behaving like a drama queen. Because all that will do is make them feel worse.

DAMAGE LIMITATION TARGETS:

15
HYPERACTIVITY – THERE'S MORE TO THIS THAN YOU MIGHT HAVE THOUGHT

Hyperactivity is pretty much guaranteed with all ADHD types. But the one thing not guaranteed is that it will be 'physical' hyperactivity.

When I had told the psychiatrist who was diagnosing me that I could be exceptionally lazy – very happy to spend hours on the sofa watching television. And I'd never climbed a tree too high or thrown myself off a garage roof in my life. He had tapped his forehead knowingly and said, 'All the hyperactivity can be in here, my dear. It can all be in here'.

That made so much sense. Because my brain doesn't stop. So the first thing to know is that hyperactivity can be all about the brain activity. Even your 'laziest layabout, won't get off her bum to do anything' ADHD teen could have a very busy brain that's hyperactive at all times. You just can't see it.

Hyperactivity can vary so much. I've seen teenagers who need to be on the go constantly. If they're not doing a sport or an activity, they will be shaking their legs vigorously, tapping their fingers, running their hands through their hair, picking finger skin, biting their nails or doing something else to keep their brain stimulated. They literally can't be still for a minute. Sometimes they hum or make sounds that they're usually not even aware of, because that stimulates their brain.

These teens are most likely to want to be out and about doing something. ANYTHING. Except be indoors which to their brain is plain BORING. Unless they're permanently attached to a device. It's these ones you really need to watch out for as they can so easily get themselves into trouble. What interests and excites them can so often be risky and thrilling – their brain just isn't interested if it isn't – and before you know it, that becomes slightly dodgy and if you're not careful, illegal.

These teens can so easily be kept on the right path if you understand just how busy they need to be! 'The devil finds work for idle hands' could have been written about ADHD teens.

I can't stress how important it is to keep your teen active, stimulated and occupied. Of the thousands of young offenders I've worked with, not one of them had hobbies. None had been encouraged to join after-school clubs, play sports, learn musical instruments, go to Girl Guides, Cubs or Scouts or dance, singing or performance-school type classes. They'd been left to their own devices and look where that got them. Behind bars. Often for the silliest, pettiest, boredom-relieving crimes like affray, fighting and pinching from shops.

So while you are never going to be able to force your ADHD teen into any particular activity, much as you might yearn for them to be a concert pianist, it has to be their choice. It's massively important you encourage them to keep searching and 'trying things out' until they find their thing.

A good example of this was one of my private client ADHD teens. He was 18/19 when I was seeing him. His mum had told me he was seriously brilliant at whatever sport he tried. He'd been told he was good enough to turn professional at football or cricket. But after a few years, both just didn't float his boat anymore. He was bored.

We spent numerous therapy sessions over nearly a year trying to find where he could focus all this physical power, skill, drive and his determination to win. I talked him out of potentially criminal activities more than once.

One day my phone rang. 'Sarah, I've FOUND IT,' he bellowed down the phone. I knew exactly what he meant so said, 'Fab. What is it?' It was boxing. He'd found an ex-Commonwealth champion boxer who had seen his potential, taken him under his wing and now he was going into London to beat the life out of anyone who dare get in the ring with him, five days a week.

I could imagine his mother's relief. She knew his constant ADHD teen inner rage and frustrations had to find an outlet. They'd nearly got him into trouble with the police more than once. But he was one of the lucky ones. He had a mum who wouldn't give up and actually gave a monkeys (the vast majority in care/prison don't) and although they'd been through some extremely rocky times when his risk-taking and thrill-seeking gave her sleepless nights, they had got there. I was over the moon for both of them. And as far as I know he's still beating the crap out of anyone he comes across. But in the ring and not on the streets!

It's generally recommended that an ADHD teen needs a minimum of one hour's exercise or activity every day. For me this was drama. I loved it. So any play rehearsal I could be at, I was there, getting my adrenaline from making people laugh and mixing with other theatrical types who were funny and made me laugh. Lots of lovely adrenaline there.

Keep it varied. Remember repetition is boring for ADHD brains. But a combo of sporting OR other after-school and weekend activities is likely to feed your ADHD teen's brain all the adrenaline it needs.

Particularly good ones are martial arts, gymnastics, boxing, cycling, horse-riding, swimming, running, skateboarding and, when you can afford it, go-karting which is a real adrenaline giver for teens.

Cricket, netball, rugby, football and team sports can be good. I was Goal Defence in my school netball team right through senior school – my ADHD heightened sense of justice and desire to win meant no imposter was getting anywhere near MY goal post. Hence I was pretty good! But beware referees who are incompetent or make bad decisions because your ADHD teen won't be able to keep quiet about that. Equally if other team members aren't pulling their weight they're soon going to know about it. ADHD teens want to win and anybody getting in the way of that … they'll soon be told just where they're going wrong. This can get particularly headstrong ADHD teens in trouble, which is why for some solo sports are better.

Always remember that keeping something on the move actually allows your teen to concentrate. So much as their tapping, shaking, fiddling or humming might drive you bonkers – it is their brain making them do it. Medication helps a lot with this.

Top Take-Aways

Hyperactivity comes with this condition. Try to accept that. And make adaptations at home that keep your ADHD teen stimulated and the rest of the family sane.

Keep them busy. An 'exhausted from sport or drama ADHD teen' is less at risk than an 'I'm sooooooo bored. I'm going out' one.

Don't Bother …

Begging them to 'just sit still for once' – it's not going to happen. It's impossible for most ADHD people.

Allowing them to miss their daily run – it's essential they get a good hour of activity a day.

DAMAGE LIMITATION TARGETS:

16
DISTRACTION – AND WHY IT'S ALWAYS GOING TO FEATURE IN AN ADHD TEEN

With ADHD teenagers distraction largely impacts in one of two ways.

The first is when they get distracted themselves and 'zone out' or 'are in their own head', 'away with the fairies' or my personal favourite 'in their butterfly brain'. This relates much more to those diagnosed with Inattentive ADHD most of whom, including my brother, tell me they spend the vast majority of their day in a permanent state of distraction.

The second is when they distract others. You may well see this in their school reports. A lot. 'Needs to focus on her own work and not distract others.' That kind of thing.

Let's start with the first. As you are hopefully getting by now, an ADHD brain needs to be stimulated to stay interested, focused and content. The minute it isn't, it's highly likely it will get distracted. This can be infuriating for parents who are keeping one eye on their teenager doing their homework, and realise that after ten minutes of solid concentration, something, either a noise, their sister barging into the room, the television being turned up louder, or literally, anything that can distract the teen's brain will have done so. 'Oi! Get on with your homework' is likely to bring a tut or an eye roll but 'How are you doing with your homework, honey?' said with enough compassion and kindness will bring the teen back to what they were doing without any bad feeling.

The most important thing to remember here is that an ADHD brain cannot help being distracted. It is on hyper-alert all the time for anything that is more interesting than what it is doing now. ADHD brains are never happy with the status quo. They always think something more exciting is round the corner. And their brain doesn't want to miss out if there is any hint of that alternative on the horizon.

For teenagers who struggle with concentrating for long periods of time without becoming distracted, it's good to factor in lots of breaks. Whatever they are doing. So whether that's homework, mowing the lawn, tidying their room or piano practice. They will find it easier to not get distracted if they know they only have to focus for 15–20 minutes, and then there is a break. When their brain can come out to play again.

Those 15–20 minutes by the way are not set in stone. Some teenagers can last for 30 or 40 minutes. As long as they know the rest of the hour can be taken up having a milkshake, some biscuits and checking their phone. Try out different time lengths to see which works best for your teenager.

Environment is also hugely important. Some teenagers get less distracted if they are in their bedroom on their own with the door shut. In fact, I would say this is the first one to try, but beware if their bedroom is chock-a-block with gadgets, televisions and iPads!

Those are going to distract even the most homework-conscientious teenagers.

Another very important thing to remember is that all people with ADHD are different when it comes to distraction. Noise is a terrible one for me. If I can hear the faintest knocking, tweeting birds, builders banging and drilling or people chattering on phones I haven't any hope of concentrating, and I'm constantly distracted till it stops.

So talking to your teenager to find out just what they need to not be distracted will likely bring very positive results. Noise cancelling headphones are something to consider, especially ones they can play music through.

But do bear in mind it's extremely difficult for an ADHD brain not to get distracted, and it's probably going to happen on a daily basis. Comments like 'why do you never listen to what I'm saying?' or 'listen to me for once in your life' are not ever helpful. They really can't help getting distracted.

Now, that age-old problem of the ADHD person distracting others!

If you haven't seen this in your ADHD teenager's school report by the time they hit their adolescence I will be very surprised. I know it was certainly in mine!

Distracting others is your teenager's way of putting dopamine into their brain. If they are bored in a class, then having a quick catch up with Mollie and how her weekend was, is going to be far more interesting than algebra.

There are ways of making it less easy to be distracted at school, college or university. One of these is sitting at the front of the class underneath the teacher's nose. Personally I would have hated this. I would have felt that I was being watched by the entire class and my anxiety would have been through the roof. I was always a 'back row girl' so I could keep an eye on what everybody was doing – and most importantly that nobody was talking about me. But I know of a lot of ADHD teenagers who actually prefer to sit right next to the teacher's desk so there is nothing in between them and what the teacher is saying to distract them. This allows a lot of ADHD kids to not get distracted and to focus purely on what the teacher is saying.

It's well worth talking to your teenager and finding out what works for them. I can't stress enough how no two ADHD teenagers are exactly the same, so what works for one may well be hell and anxiety-giving for another. So communication is key. Find out what it is they need to be able to concentrate and not get distracted and don't give up at the first attempt. Be prepared to try out different methods.

Top Take-Aways

An ADHD brain cannot help becoming distracted. It's part of the brain wiring and the only thing that matters is how you deal with it.

Remember you are always trying to keep your ADHD teenager's self-esteem intact. So any positive ways of managing distraction are always going to be better than making them feel bad about something they genuinely can't help.

Don't Bother …

Expecting to eradicate distraction. It's always going to be there in some shape or form. Working with your teenager to find ways of managing it is the way to go.

DAMAGE LIMITATION TARGETS:

17
IMPULSIVITY – AND WHY THOSE 11 LITTLE LETTERS SPELL DANGER!

Impulsivity quite simply means doing or saying anything without thinking. Before it's diagnosed or medicated an ADHD brain does pretty much everything impulsively. This can get us into some dreadful and dangerous situations and I will use one of mine as an example to show you just how much!

Many moons ago I was sitting in a cinema and the people in front of me were talking. Despite my regular shushing and kicking the back of the chair, they just did not stop. Constant talking, totally distracting me from watching the film.

Before I tell you what I did next, it's important for you to know that I had absolutely no idea this was going to happen. This was not planned. I didn't think about it. I certainly didn't think of any consequence. But before I knew anything was happening, I had reached down, pulled this person out of their seat by the lapels of their jacket and screamed in their face to 'SHUT THE F*CK UP,' and then literally threw them back down into their seat.

I don't know who was more shocked: me, them or the friend I was sitting next to, whose eyes opened wide with a look of absolute horror.

I couldn't explain it myself until thirty years later, when I was diagnosed ADHD and I realised THIS is what impulsivity is. Literally not thinking before you take an action or say anything.

I just thank the Lord this was in the days before people more commonly carried knives or guns, because I'm quite sure if I did that now I would find myself in the local A&E if I was lucky. Less lucky – the mortuary. I really did throw her back down with a terrible force.

Impulsivity can be responsible for many teenagers getting into so much trouble and is one of the main reasons I encourage parents to either consider or reconsider medication. Taking ADHD medication reduces and sometimes completely eradicates impulsivity and, very importantly, allows an ADHD brain to think of the consequences. My brain did not think of the consequences when I threw that girl back in her seat. Today it would, because I am on ADHD medication.

Some teenagers are incredibly impulsive. They will walk out the door in the morning and have not a clue where they are going or what they are going to do. Things might go well for them or they may not. If a police officer happens to get in their way, asking annoying questions, they might impulsively tell them to 'f*ck off' and before they know it find themselves in a police cell.

I can't begin to tell you how many ADHD teenagers I have worked with who have found themselves in trouble because of their impulsivity. Here are just a few classic examples.

- Arrested for 'threats to kill' when she didn't like the way a girl was treating her ex-boyfriend and impulsively told her she 'would kill her' if she found out she had been unfaithful to him.

- Impulsively attacked a gang of ten much younger boys who had been bullying and had beaten up his younger brother. Arrested for affray and criminal damage.

- Impulsively threw 4,000 invoices in the air and told her boss to 'stick her job where the sun don't shine' the day before payday and a week before her rent was due.

- Impulsively bought a flat in Bulgaria, after seeing it advertised in a newspaper, and lost £30,000. Oops, that was me!

You can see where I'm going with this. Impulsivity can get teens into trouble with teachers at school, parents at home, anybody in authority and even with the law. And the very frustrating thing is we have little control over it. And it really is one of the very best reasons for trying to get your teenager to at least try ADHD medication.

ADHD medication has the wonderful effect of allowing you to think of the consequences. It's quite breathtaking when you first take it and you realise that in your entire life you have not actually thought of the consequences of anything. I remember the first time I took it in my mid 50s, and suddenly thinking of the consequences was quite spooky, never having done so before.

Spending money is something your ADHD teenager is likely to do impulsively. So many traits lead into this. ADHD people don't have the patience to wait for birthdays or Christmas. If they've decided they want something, they want it now, so they will impulsively go and spend their last Christmas money on some almost identical trainers to the ones they own.

Or worse, if they have already spent that money, they will possibly pinch them and hope they won't get caught.

This is another reason to encourage your ADHD teenager to work from a young age. If they have their own money, they are far less likely to take things impulsively because they will know in a couple of weeks they will actually have the money to buy them anyway.

Speaking impulsively is a huge problem for ADHD people – words genuinely will come out of our mouths before we've given them any thought whatsoever. I have lost probably three or four very good friends over the years because I have impulsively said something that has offended them. A couple of those friends I don't mind losing, but a couple of them I really did. But my impulsive mouth got the better of me.

Another way ADHD teens can impulsively take action and get themselves into trouble is by being dared to do things by friends. No self-respecting ADHD teen is EVER going to say no to a dare, so very often they will impulsively say 'course I'd do it' before impulsively throwing themselves off a bridge into Lord knows how deep a river.

Many ADHD teenagers will impulsively tell a brother or sister that they are going to stab them in their sleep, chop their arms off or bury them alive. These words will pour out of their mouth with absolutely no thought. Terrifying as this might be for the sibling, it's best that you educate the brother or sister in how impulsive your ADHD teen might be, and how they shouldn't take every single thing that comes out of their mouth as gospel.

For the impulsive ADHD child, they will have literally forgotten what they said two minutes later. So there's no need for your sibling to lie quaking in their bed that night terrified that little sister is on her way, brandishing a circular saw.

Impulsivity is responsible for a large portion of the juvenile prison and Young Offender Institute population. So many of the boys in there have done things impulsively and ended up breaking the law completely unintentionally. It's quite heartbreaking listening to their stories, because it's very obvious if they had been on ADHD medication they wouldn't have made most, if not all, of the decisions they made.

Needing excitement and adrenaline leads to impulsivity. So while your 13-year-old might have been out for a walk with his mates along the river, if there is suddenly a high rocky ledge to dive into that river, guess which of those children is going to impulsively throw himself off that rock? You've got it. The ADHD one.

There really aren't any magic answers to dealing with impulsivity apart from ADHD medication, which is why it's always worth trying more than one and not giving up even if there are some side-effects.

Having a grown-up conversation with your teenager, literally when they start senior school, is a very good idea. If they understand what impulsivity actually is, what sort of behaviour it could lead to, and what sort of trouble it can get them into, it will help them make better decisions and choices. It won't make them infallible but being aware of the dangers of impulsivity will definitely help them.

Top Take-Aways

Impulsivity comes with ADHD. If a teenager isn't medicated, be very wary of what they get up to impulsively and make sure they have a thorough understanding of what impulsivity means. The more they know, the more they are going to be alert to dangerous situations.

Don't Bother …

Reacting to every single thing that comes out of your ADHD teenager's mouth. So much of it will have been impulsive and immediately forgotten by the teen.

Focus on battles worth fighting; trying to stop them being impulsive, during puberty, without medication, is not a battle you are going to win!

DAMAGE LIMITATION TARGETS:

18
BOREDOM – AND WHY YOU NEED TO AVOID IT LIKE THE PLAGUE

Boredom is something to be avoided at all costs, because a bored ADHD teenager is an at-risk ADHD teenager.

Boredom is sheer torture to an ADHD brain, which is constantly looking for stimulation and to replace the dopamine it lacks. So keeping your ADHD teenager engaged in whatever tickles their fancy is VERY important.

I remember during school holidays in my early teens always going into my mother's bedroom first thing and asking what was happening that day. If she said, 'Nothing. It's an at-home day,' my heart fell into my boots. I would literally feel a wave of low mood wash over me.

Whereas if she said, 'Well you've got the morning to yourself, but this afternoon we're going shopping and then we're going swimming,' my heart would swell. I knew there was something happening, something exciting, something to look forward to and I could therefore fill up my morning with things I wanted to get done, knowing I had lovely things to look forward to in the afternoon.

On a day when there was nothing to do I would be grumpy. Nothing would interest me. All the usual things I would get up to in my bedroom like playing music, reading books and magazines, doing my homework, all completely lost my interest because I was bored with nothing to look forward to.

So keeping your ADHD teenager busy, active, and preferably doing something where there is a reward at the end of it, is your absolute goal.

I strongly recommend you have something lined up at weekends where you are out of the house and doing something. If your teenager is into a sport, that's nice and easy. If they aren't then family swimming, climbing, bowling, football or rounders in the park in the summer or some other outdoor activity is highly recommended.

As they get older in their teens, they won't want to be involved in this stuff but early teens it's definitely a great idea to get them out of the house both days at the weekend doing something physical that they actually enjoy. Cycling is another good one. If you have a child who loves their bike then going off cycling for a couple of hours each day is a great idea. I remember playing numerous catching-a-ball games with my dad and stepmum and being able to amuse myself for hours just with a ball in the park.

On rainy days and wintry days it's harder. Once homework is done, and if your teen is going out of their mind with boredom, allow them on their devices. This is something parents have a huge problem with and the battles I've seen in families over devices – I could write an entire book on those.

What you have to remember is, with ADHD teenagers, devices fulfil so many roles. They are brightly coloured, constantly moving and easily swiped onto the next thing if something gets boring. They can be educational, competitive if they are playing games to fulfil their need for winning, and the stimulation also calms their brain down.

Speaking with a client recently, she was allowing her teenager 45 minutes a day on the iPad. She was quite shocked to hear that I know other parents who feel they are doing well if they can get their son or daughter off an iPad within five hours!

There are no set rules with this. Each parent will have their own ideas and their own boundaries, but my view on it is quite clear and based on a lot of ADHD teenage clients! If your teen is in the house, safe, where you know they are, amusing themselves quite legally, happy, with their brain being beautifully stimulated – you have nothing to worry about. It's a darn sight safer than them being out, you not knowing where they are, who they are mixing with, what drugs they might be offered and what petty crime they might be being coerced or threatened to get involved in. Devices are the least of your worries when that's the choice.

And I speak from family experience of this. When my middle brother was aged around 13, he and his group of friends were coerced into travelling into the next big town to steal videos and CDs by older boys at his school. Of course he was caught by the police. My mother was mortified and angry.

The biggest boredom busters of our age most definitely come in the shape of FIFA, Xbox, PlayStations, iPads and the like. And because the alternative is nearly always riskier, I personally don't think there is a lot to be gained from banning your teenager using devices when most often they are then going to be angry, slam out of the house and go and get themselves involved in who knows what.

It's always a good idea to have a stack of games, playing cards, art and craft materials and anything you can think of for when your teenagers do need to stay in. It's not very often they are going to want to sit down and play Monopoly with Dad and Uncle Pete, but just sometimes they might want to. It has to be their choice though.

And encourage your teenager to have as many interests as possible. You won't be able to force these on them. It will need to be their decision. But whether they get their buzz from playing cricket, go-karting, knitting, writing poetry, having singing lessons, visiting their nan to play with her dog, or whatever it happens to be – encourage them to be active, and ideally to have one activity after school each day. Not quite so necessary if they've had sport/PE classes during the day but having something to do after school is usually a good idea. A knackered ADHD teenager is one who is less likely to get into trouble.

Their brothers and sisters will also be grateful for you keeping the ADHD one occupied. Otherwise they will find their bored sibling interfering with what they are doing, 'wanting to play too' until ten minutes later when they're bored and running off to pastures new.

It's no good telling your ADHD teen off for aggravating their sister or brother unless you've actually found them something else more stimulating to occupy their mind. Annoying people on purpose can be great fun for an ADHD teenager.

Top Take-Aways

Boredom comes with the ADHD territory. Don't expect your child to be able to sit, relax and do nothing. Their brain demands more from them than that.

So be prepared to keep them active, engaged and busy with whatever activities motivate and excite them. You might need to suggest options to them, but always let the decision be theirs.

Don't Bother ...

Telling them that 'they can't be bored, they had a very busy day yesterday'. It doesn't work like that. Their brain is constantly looking for something fun and exciting to do.

And never push them into things they aren't interested in. However hard you push it's not going to work. If it is not something they are passionate about, even if the whole family has played rugby going back to 1848 – if your son hates rugby, it's just not going to happen.

My undiagnosed ADHD niece, who was the best street dancer I'd ever seen aged 5 to 11, then decided she didn't like it, abruptly stopped her classes and despite much pleading from many family members has refused to go near it since. Save your energy!

DAMAGE LIMITATION TARGETS:

19
NOT-QUITE-TELLING-THE-TRUTH TO BLATANT LYING!

Whenever I talk about this, it brings out very strong reactions in people. Some clients look at me, disgustedly, saying, 'I have never told a lie in my life'.

Other parents weep with relief, when they realise that their child's constant twisting the truth and telling outright lies is not unusual in ADHD children, adolescents and even adults.

I firmly believe this is yet another trait that ramps up during puberty. And from my own brain and the research I've done with clients, I believe these are the main reasons that children in particular (but there are some adults that carry it on), twist the truth and sometimes tell blatant lies.

- To liven things up. ADHD people, especially teenagers, can find life quite mundane. So if they can add a few arms and legs onto a story to make it sound more interesting, they will do. And sometimes they will tell outright lies purely to make something sound more interesting. One of my own examples was going into school one morning and explaining my late arrival from the GP's by telling the entire class that a man had dropped dead in the surgery waiting room that morning. I was found out later the same day when somebody asked my mother about it. Looking back, I think this was to cover up anxiety because I was later back than expected, and also to make myself a little bit more interesting that day to everybody else!

- To get something we want. Once an ADHD teenager has decided they want something e.g. a new phone, their brain will not be able to let it rest until they get that new phone. So this is when they slip in the odd lie to help their brain get what it wants, e.g., 'My phone is just not working, Mum. I know it looks like it is now, but every now and again it flashes and it goes off and I desperately need it for school work,' said with big teary eyes.

- To feed the compulsive brain. I was fabulous at this. The amount of times I told my mother, 'We only had a very small salad at lunchtime so I need a big tea,' and it worked every time. I also used to pinch money out of her purse to buy food from the swimming pool snack machine. So lying about food intake and how much more is needed is pretty common! I'm not proud of it now, but I was only about 12 at the time.

- To hide risky behaviour. Of course all teenagers do this, but I suspect ADHD teenagers do it more than most. Your son will tell you that 'of course his friend's parents are going to be in the whole evening' that he wants to spend at his mate James' house – when James' mother and father have already planned a romantic date night at the local Italian. This can go from the minorly annoying to the majorly worrying. Because your teen could be out doing anything and everything when you think they are being watched over by other parents.

- Impulsivity and literally not thinking before words pour out of their mouth. Bearing in mind an unmedicated ADHD brain is always impulsive, your teen may have come out with a whopper lie before they've genuinely given themselves five seconds to think it through. And then they'll panic, knowing they've got themselves into a hole with no clue how to get out.

- Because we most often have a shocking short-term memory and can genuinely think we've done something when we haven't. Telling you they have brushed their teeth when they haven't been within a country mile of the bathroom that morning could actually be because they've genuinely forgotten.

- To impress or 'keep up' with their mates. If all their friends have smoked, tried cannabis, or drunk alcohol, your teen will not want to be seen as different or – God forbid – 'uncool' so instead they'll lie to save face.

These are the main motivators behind the choice to not to tell the truth, in my opinion – and having worked with hundreds of teenagers adept at lying!

It's one of the traits I do stress needs addressing though. Of course we accept that short-term memory means ADHD teens are going to say something that isn't true, but that's a genuine mistake and most definitely doesn't need any sort of punishment. Perhaps it flags up something that does need handling differently, though, for example, Post-it note reminders to do things like brushing teeth and not forgetting to take homework in can be extremely useful.

But the genuine lying, usually for gain, or to get out of doing something, does need to be dealt with and the earlier the better. So as soon as you catch your teenager telling lies or, as I prefer to call it, 'not telling the truth', it's time to have a very serious chat with them.

This chat might even be pre-teen years as it's not unheard of for ADHD children to start lying from the age of 4 or 5 onwards. So whatever age they are, I suggest you handle it this way.

Firstly, have this conversation with them in private, away from other siblings or parents, and most definitely when they're in the right frame of mind. This won't be when they are hungry, tired, have just come in from school, have had a row with their sister/brother or are grumpy for any other reason.

So catch them when they are in a good mood, and you can speak to them without risk of being overheard.

You don't need to dwell on the incident. If you and they both know exactly what they have done, don't go over it and berate them and make them feel worse.

The important bit is that they now tell you the truth. Before you get started, let them know that they won't be judged, told off or punished for what they have done, because you understand that especially during puberty, not telling the truth can be a problem for some ADHD teenagers. Make sure they understand that you realise this is part and parcel of their ADHD condition and you are not judging them for it BUT together you do have to come up with a plan because you don't want them getting into trouble in future.

Make it very clear that this is because you want to protect them, you don't want them getting into trouble and very importantly you are ON THEIR SIDE. I can't begin to tell you how critical that bit is.

Give them age-appropriate examples where lying has led people into trouble. You might have your own family examples, but if not, you can use celebrities who have not told the truth and then lost their job or athletes who have not told the truth about taking performance-enhancing medication. If you can use ADHD celebrity or athlete examples even better.

Once they've understood the fact that lying is not the best idea, and it could get them into serious trouble, you need to have a plan in place for how they deal with it if they 'mistakenly don't tell the truth again in the future.' And I strongly suggest that's how you word it.

How they do this is for you and your child to decide. The best idea I know of that has worked with other teenagers is this one: having a 24- or 48-hour window where they can admit the truth to you, and they will not receive any sort of punishment or judgment.

If you opt for this make sure you both know how they can do that. Suggestions would be an email, a text, a note under your bedroom door or something else confidential where they won't face humiliation. And other siblings won't be privy to that information.

Don't forget, your teenager will most probably have 'not told the truth' impulsively and without thinking of the consequences. Pretty soon after they have done it, they will realise that it wasn't the brightest idea, so if you give them a route OUT of the lie, most ADHD teenagers will take it.

If and when they do take it, make sure you praise them hugely. Thank them for telling the truth, reaffirm that they have done absolutely the right thing, you are very grateful to them and you are proud of them. The more they hear of this, the more likely they are to come clean the next time.

There will be blips. Make sure they know this. You aren't expecting them to change overnight, but as long as they aim to be truthful within that time frame, they are moving in the right direction. The very fact they know there will be blips means there will be less of them, in my experience.

Some ADHD teens take lying to the next level. I know because I've met them. Sadly, I've met them behind bars because consistent liars do often end up in the criminal justice system.

So impressing on your adolescent the need for them to be truthful, however painful the truth is, really is critical for their future.

Top Take-Aways

Don't be surprised if your ADHD teenager begins lying when they start puberty. Also, don't be surprised if they have started lying before that! Aged 4 is the youngest I have witnessed. It's not a sign they are on the road to ruin. It's part of their ADHD, and all that matters is how you handle it.

Don't Bother ...

Threatening them or punishing them for telling lies. Certainly don't humiliate them in front of other people for not having told the truth. That's not going to move you forward at all.

Understanding, explaining the connection with ADHD and having a firm plan in place for when they don't tell the truth immediately works much better.

DAMAGE LIMITATION TARGETS:

20
PROCRASTINATION – AND WHY THEY COULD PROBABLY WIN A MEDAL FOR IT

Procrastination is a very big ADHD trait. As always, some people have it very mildly, and I would put myself in that category, and then there are others who have it so severely it completely cripples their life. So the important question is, first of all, if your teenager is procrastinating, we need to know WHY. Then I can give you the best ways I know of managing each.

Firstly, and in so many cases, procrastination is caused by a lack of motivation to do something. This will be for one overriding reason, and that is – it is just not stimulating enough for the ADHD brain. You may well have thought it's just your teenager being a terrible time-waster, when actually it's their brain not being stimulated enough to propel them into any sort of action. Honestly!

ADHD brains are reward based. This means they function better when there is a nice, big, fat juicy reward at the end of whatever it is the brain is being asked to do. So getting up, getting showered, brushing teeth, getting dressed and then going into school is unlikely to motivate most ADHD teenagers. There's not much juicy and exciting about going into the same old school with the same old teachers, doing the same old lessons. Especially if it's the same old story of their ADHD not having been recognised or diagnosed and the same old story of nobody spotting their coexisting conditions!

They might be struggling every day to appear competent and not stand out, so being motivated to go in and force yourself to do that daily is going to be exceptionally hard. Dragging themselves from their pit and into the shower is going to feel like the most momentous, effort-requiring task on the planet. Going into school is not usually exciting enough to stimulate an ADHD brain!

Other things that don't generally excite an ADHD brain are doing homework, tidying up their room, sorting out their school bag, washing, showering, bathing or 'ablutions' of any kind (I just love that word, ablutions) including cleaning teeth – and most kids are expected to do that TWICE A DAY! Pure torture!

All this repetitive stuff that needs to be done EVERY day is utterly uninspiring for an ADHD brain. Hence why I have had more stinky teenagers in my therapy room than most. A lot of these teenagers, like me, decided that cleaning teeth and showering just really wasn't worth their valuable time and gave it up for a chunk of their teenage years.

I decided that cleaning my teeth at one point really was absolutely unnecessary so I stopped. Completely. I think I was about 12 or maybe 13. The next time I went to the dentist I had to have four fillings! With a pain threshold as low as mine, I made very sure I cleaned my teeth from that day onwards. I also went through a patch of deciding bathing was desperately dull so would run a bath and then sit on a chair next to it reading a book. I don't think it was that long before someone pointed out I was smelling less than fragrant.

So lack of motivation causing procrastination is definitely reason number one.

Reason number two, believe it or not, is perfectionism. There are some people who have perfectionism so severely that they won't get started on something because they fear not doing it perfectly. I've met quite a few of these people and this can be a very serious issue.

I knew a lovely ADHD man once who had spent twenty years preparing his new business but had yet to deal with any customers because he wasn't sure he could do it exactly as he wanted. This was an intelligent, clever man with a PhD, and it drove his wife literally round the twist that he could never get started. In the end, she started up and ran his business for him, but that still didn't motivate him to get going. He was perpetually worried that he wasn't going to be able to do things perfectly, so he just couldn't get off the starting block.

The third main reason teens procrastinate, in my experience, is because they don't want to make a fool of themselves. And if we take into account Rejection Sensitive Dysphoria, there are a lot of teenagers who are putting off doing something at school, or doing homework, because they don't quite know what they're doing and they don't want to look an idiot for getting it wrong. So procrastination can sometimes be due to anxiety and fear of humiliation.

These are the only reasons I have come across as to why teenagers procrastinate. I don't want to make light of this because it can be very serious and it can drive parents absolutely potty. If their teenager answers every single request with 'yes in a minute' or 'yes later' or 'I'll do it tomorrow' – and this can go on for years – you can see why parents get to screaming point.

Putting things off can become seriously life impacting. There are relationships that collapse because ADHD partners put off proposing, buying a house together or having children.

So before those issues impact them in adulthood, it's a very good idea to sit down with your teen and have a serious conversation about procrastination. Explain to them that it is a trait of ADHD and is due to their wonderfully different brain wiring. You need to find out exactly why they do it. If it's purely because things are too boring, then together you have to come up with ways of making them more exciting.

Because the whole bathing, showering, cleaning teeth combo is one of the main problems, let's tackle that first. A very good way to make that more exciting is to get a Bluetooth radio in the bathroom, so your teenager can sing along to whatever music they like. A waterproof television also goes a long way if you can afford it, but definitely something that will entertain them while they are in the bath or shower.

Other ways to motivate them, especially in the morning, is to offer some sort of reward. If they are up, showered, teeth cleaned, dressed and downstairs by 8 a.m., they will get something that will inspire them. Maybe it's their choice of how their eggs are done, or they get a fried breakfast if they are ready on time, or bacon/sausage sandwiches or something that will get them down the stairs ready for school – because there's something enticing enough at the bottom of the stairs.

Many parents have used a lift to school as the reward for being downstairs ready for school on time. Otherwise, the teenager has to walk or get the bus.

They will need a reason to motivate themselves to get out of bed, dressed and downstairs at the right time. Every teen will be different and will be motivated by something specific to them, so you might need to be creative and flexible. It's worth persevering because their brain will always be reward based so something WILL always motivate them. You've just got to find it!

One thing I would be very wary of with ADHD teenagers – and I have seen so many parents fall into this trap – is thinking it's just easier to do it yourself. These parents tend to take on a lot of the chores the teenagers should be doing and feel that for a quiet life it's just much easier if they get on and do it themselves. I don't recommend this route because it turns teenagers into lazy adults who expect people to do everything for them and, in turn, into terrible partners/husbands/wives.

Much better is to find out why they procrastinate, what they really loathe and despise doing, and then find something that will motivate them into doing it. It's actually quite simple if you remember that their brain is reward based and always will be.

For ADHD teens who procrastinate because they are perfectionists, this is trickier. These kids will have anxiety and if they aren't on meds it's something that ADHD medication will help. Perfectionism is again a very serious issue. I am diagnosed with it myself, and for some of us with ADHD it's one of the worst elements of the condition.

Perfectionists need careful handling. Again communication is key. Find out what they need to be perfect for them to function. It will be different for absolutely everybody. But if you take their condition seriously and show that you are doing everything to make things possible for them, it should help them get started.

ADHD teens can get very overwhelmed so doing things in small chunks is always a good idea. If you have a perfectionist who is procrastinating starting on a massive project, suggest they begin with just one thing. Maybe choose a diagram they need to draw and just do that. Break it down into small bite-size chunks then they can do each one individually and perfectly before they move onto the next.

If you are lucky, you might swerve all of this, because your teenager might be one of those with the 'ADHD internal motor'. This means that they need to do everything now, quickly and can't put anything off or wait until tomorrow. If you've one of those teens, you hopefully won't find procrastination too much of a problem. Exhausting themselves and never stopping will bring issues of their own, but it won't bring procrastination often unless something is exceptionally boring.

Top Take-Aways

Procrastination is part of having ADHD. Accept that it is an element of their condition, it won't just naturally evaporate, and you have to find ways of managing it. Remember the ADHD teen's brain is reward based and incorporating some kind of reward system is most likely to work.

Perfectionism needs specific handling and is a serious condition which can be debilitating.

Don't Bother ...

Shouting at them, threatening to withdraw screen time or docking pocket money, humiliating them or telling them to 'just get on with it'. That will get you nowhere, apart from both of you angry and frustrated.

DAMAGE LIMITATION TARGETS:

21
DISORGANISATION – AND WHY IT MIGHT DRIVE YOU INSANE

If you are the kind of parents who like your house neat, tidy with everything in its right place at all times and you have a whirling dervish of a chaotic ADHD teenager living in your house, I send you my very deepest sympathies. I have an ADHD partner who lives in utter chaos, so I genuinely feel your pain.

I am one of those rare (but we do exist) ADHD people in that I have an actual diagnosis of 'perfectionism'. For the vast majority of ADHD teenagers who don't have perfectionism, you are going to be dealing with disorganisation in just about every area of their life. And if it drives you round the twist, I promise you I understand because my partner's disorganisation drives me literally bonkers. I'd go further than that. I would say it actually makes me ill. I cannot bear the chaos and mess he lives in all the time so you really do have my sympathy here.

So first, let's have a look at where this comes from. ADHD brains are very often likened to Spaghetti Junction. There's an awful lot of activity going on in there, all the time, and any element of orderliness, being in control, cool, calm and collected doesn't very often feature. So as our brains work in a chaotic way, it's only the natural progression that we operate in a chaotic and disorganised way.

Those of us with perfectionism fight this constantly, which is absolutely exhausting, because even *we* have chaotic brains and naturally lean towards disorganised living, but we fight it 24/7 because we cannot stand mess and can't actually function in chaos.

But for an average ADHD teenager being organised is just something that doesn't interest them much and is usually too far out of reach for them to consider worth even attempting. Disorganisation can affect them in so many ways and it can seriously impact on their education, friendships, sibling relationships and, believe it or not, their own mental wellbeing, so it is something we need to take quite seriously.

Firstly, let's take school. Their disorganisation might impact on them not knowing what day of the week it is, let alone what lessons are coming up. So making sure they're taking in the right textbooks, PE kits or homework is going to be challenge number one. Never mind the fact that they may well lose what they need for particular lessons, even on their way to school. Trust me, with ADHD, this happens!

There are some very good tried and tested ways around ADHD disorganisation, the first of which is Post-it notes. Post-it notes work extremely well for ADHD brains because they are compact, different vibrant colours, movable and throw-away-able.

When your teen was younger, it would have been appropriate for you to remind them each day what they needed to take in to school and to help pack their school bag. Now they are in their teen years and adolescence, I strongly recommend you start to encourage them to take responsibility for this sort of stuff themselves. But they are going to need help with organising it initially. Your first port of call is Post-it notes! Also often very useful are alarms on their phone.

Post-it notes are great because you can have one for each day. So Monday, for example, might say -

- Need netball kit

- Take ingredients for food tech

- Need to bring English homework home

- Netball practice, 4 pm to 5 pm

This little but important Post-it note should be where they will always see it in the morning, so perhaps on their bedside table, dressing table, or wherever their school uniform is laid out. And once all the morning activities have been achieved, it needs to be popped into their school bag and for them to get in the habit of checking the note before they come home from school. That way the English homework won't get forgotten and they will make it to netball practice.

I totally understand that remembering to check that Post-it note can be a problem, so if you have a kind teacher to prod them – even better! Teens who have a locker at school often have these Post-it notes stuck to the inside of the locker door, so that each day they see exactly what they need to take home with them. Yes, there is always the chance they won't look at the locker door, but if you keep up with the system it's generally a winner.

Alarms on their phone, if they are allowed them after school, also work extremely well. You can label alarms on phones so each day it can remind them what they need to bring home from school. And for those who are doing after-school activities, exactly where they've got to be and at what time that day. I'm not joking when I say an ADHD person might not even know what day it is. I spend half my life asking people what day it is because I can never remember. So don't assume your teen will know what day it is, let alone what they are supposed to be doing. The phone is a very handy reminder for what the date is, what the day is and what they are supposed to be doing.

For school you can adapt systems if they struggle with something in particular. So let's say forgetting PE kit is a constant nightmare in your house. Have two of them: one that they keep at school all the time, and on any day they are playing netball a second one is taken in and left in the locker, so it is ready for next time. These are called 'reasonable adjustments' and they are what people with conditions like ADHD need. Yes it might cost you the price of a second netball kit, but it's worth it if there is always one at school, one in the wash and you don't have the weekly panic because they have forgotten it.

A whiteboard at home can also be quite useful. Again with the day at the top, what needs to go in to school, what needs to come home and any after-school activity timings and locations.

Always remember that ADHD people have very poor short-term memories so holding something in our head is always going to be difficult. Having it written down and visible is going to take the stress and worry out of that situation. Your teen will worry what they'll forget so a good, solid reminder system will remove that worry.

Now let's have a look at disorganisation at home. You have lots of ADHD traits here clashing with each other. Remember we like to buy things – giving us that much-needed adrenaline boost. We impulsively like purchasing new things and that can very easily lead to owning an overwhelming load of rubbish that we don't actually want or need and often nowhere to put it. So the first thing is to try to rein your teen in from buying everything they think they want. Once you have that under control you need to tackle whatever 'stuff' they already have in their room.

If we are dealing with a bomb site to begin with, you first need to have a very good clear out. I would suggest three bin liners. One that you put rubbish in, one that is good enough quality to go to the charity shop and one for items that you/they want to keep.

Always remember that ADHD people have more compassion than most. So stress upon your teenager that the charity shop bag is going to help teens who cannot afford to have three PlayStations and twelve Nike tracksuits. There's a higher chance of them letting some of them go if they believe they're going to other teenagers who have no hope of affording them otherwise.

Then it's a question of organising what you are left with. Before we start thinking about storage, something to know is that with ADHD people of any age, there is a saying – and it's very true – 'if we can't see it, it doesn't exist'.

So think long and hard about the best storage options for your teenager.

I would dispense with the idea of very high-tech sophisticated wardrobe systems where you have to press a button for a door to open. Something as slow as that is going to frustrate your teenager. They are going to want something quick and easy that takes minimal effort.

Shelving and baskets are my best suggestion. Anything put away in a wardrobe is unlikely ever to be seen again. Your teenager will only use the top three or four things in any pile and never bother to look further down. I say 'teenager'; I still do this to this day!

So if you can come up with some nice shelving units where their clothes can be stored so they can actually SEE them, that's ideal. And baskets are also an extremely good idea. The sort that you can tuck neatly in an IKEA unit. If they can have one basket for pants, one for socks, one for T-shirts, that sort of thing, they are likely to get used. And clothes likely to be put away.

As for dirty washing. That needs to be an open basket or linen style container where they can literally chuck their dirty clothes in without the effort of opening a lid. Otherwise it is guaranteed to end up on the floor.

Much as impulsive buying and wanting the best of everything is part of ADHD, I strongly urge you to try to keep your teenager's belongings – and that includes clothes, trainers, shoes and boots – down to as minimal a level as they will let you. It's so easy for ADHD teenagers to become overwhelmed and not be able to cope. By keeping things simple and to a minimum their life really does work much better.

When I have a good clear out of my clothes, fill up a few bin liners and take them to the charity shop, I can't begin to tell you the weight that lifts off my shoulders. I feel I can breathe again. And this is how it will be for your teenager.

We know ADHD people don't like being told what to do, and teenagers especially, so I strongly suggest you collaboratively chat to your teenager about what would work best for them when it comes to organising school bags, what goes in and out of school, and how they would like to organise their room. Some of them won't know these little ADHD idiosyncrasies like 'if we can't see it, it doesn't exist', so you'll need to explain this to them and find ways that work for your particular teenager.

Top Take-Aways

Disorganisation is part of the ADHD condition. It's highly unlikely you will have a naturally organised adolescent on your hands. Don't berate them or humiliate them for their untidiness, but work together to find different ways of being organised that work for them.

Don't Bother …

Doing it all for them in the hope they will watch what you do and copy you. They won't. They'll just be glad that they have got away with not doing it.

They need to learn how to organise themselves as they get older, especially as they start to think about leaving home or going away to college or university. So putting in systems now that work will help them when they have to start taking responsibility for themselves.

DAMAGE LIMITATION TARGETS:

22
RISK-TAKING AND THRILL-SEEKING – PAY EXTRA ATTENTION TO THIS CHAPTER BECAUSE IT COULD SAVE YOU A LOT OF HEARTACHE

It's funny how this trait doesn't get talked about much when people go through lists of ADHD traits, but in actual fact it's a massive part of ADHD for so many reasons.

Firstly, it's how we get our adrenaline, and our brains crave adrenaline constantly.

Secondly, it plays a major part in keeping ADHD people happy. If we aren't finding something thrilling or exciting, then we are very probably bored and most certainly looking for something thrilling or exciting, which often comes by taking risks. This can be extremely dangerous. For example: fire. A lot of ADHD teens find fire fascinating. I've actually met ADHD adults who, as children, have been taken into care due to their love of starting fires. And I've met others arrested for arson.

Thirdly, it's one of the main traits that draws teenagers into trouble, sometimes with parents and teachers, but potentially also the police, so it needs a LOT of attention.

The good news is there are ways of managing this constant need for risky and exciting activities, but the very important thing is you understand and accept that it IS going to be there and it needs to be managed, especially during puberty when this trait is at its most heightened.

There are a very small minority of ADHD teenagers who have told me over the years that they have never done anything faintly risky or thrill-seeking, and these are always the ones who have anxiety. Anxiety has held them back. Numerous teen clients have told me that they would have done something, 'but they were worried they would hurt themselves", 'they were worried they would get in trouble' or they had over-thought it to the point that it didn't become exciting anymore. But this is a very small percentage. The rest are on the lookout for something exciting or risky a lot of the time, especially when they aren't occupied doing something stimulating enough.

So keeping your teen occupied and busy is crucial. Allowing a teenager to be regularly bored or understimulated doesn't mean they're going to sit down nicely and read a book for a few days. It means they will slam the front door, most probably flinging an 'I'm soooo BORED I'm going out' over their shoulder as they disappear.

So if we accept most ADHD people take risks and seek thrills, and that during their adolescent years your teenager is going to want to do this a lot more, how on earth do we fulfil that constant need for thrills?! I have good news for you. I've worked with thousands of these teenagers, and I can tell you some of the ways they have found their thrills and had their adrenaline-seeking satisfied! In VERY many different ways.

Let's start with the easy one. Sport. If you have a girl or a boy ADHD teenager who is interested in sport, half your work has just been done for you. Encourage them to try different sports, because if your son is good at cricket he may well be good at anything else that involves hitting a ball. If your daughter is good at netball, encourage her to have a go at basketball or anything else where she is chucking a ball through a hoop.

It's very rare for a child who is sporty to be good at only one sport. So encourage them to try different adrenaline-giving sports. Some that work particularly well are go-karting, bicycle riding, wall/rock climbing, swimming, diving, martial arts and boxing. That's not to eliminate the rest, but I know a lot of ADHD kids who throw themselves into one of these activities and go very far with it, representing the school, then the county and some of them even their country.

And then, for your boys and girls who prefer team sports, let them have taster sessions at football, rugby, cricket, golf and anything else available in your area. You might be surprised when your child who shows absolutely no aptitude for anything, suddenly becomes alive and desperate to win when they are on a badminton court. So keep introducing them to different sports because you may well be very surprised by what appeals to them.

When I was in my early teens I belonged to a table tennis club. I don't even know if they exist anymore. But I absolutely adored my Saturday afternoons spent bashing balls on the table and was incredibly competitive. I definitely found my adrenaline that way.

Running and athletics is another sport ADHD teenagers can be very good at. I've had clients before, aged 13, who were running with 16-year-olds because they were so fast. Our desire to win is very strong, so see if your teenager likes running or hurdling, long jump, high jump, anything like that.

Those of you who live near the sea, rivers, lakes or water of any kind, you also have all the water options. Waterskiing is a huge adrenaline giver and I've known many ADHD kids get into windsailing, scuba-diving and wild water swimming. One family even bought a boat, as they were on the coast, and took their very active son sailing every weekend, which he found thrilling AND exhausting meaning he slept much better. Win-win situation.

For kids who aren't sporty, look at the performing arts. These can come in all sorts of shapes and sizes. Your child might want to go to a stage school part-time where they learn singing, dance and drama. Or they might want to specialise in purely singing, have lessons and join a choir or even form a band.

Dance lessons is another brilliant way to get adrenaline. Street dance classes, ballet, tap, jazz, whatever floats their boat. For me, it was drama and comedy and I was in every school play. I joined an amateur dramatic group as soon as I could. Making a crowd laugh and hearing people clap at my performance was probably still the biggest adrenaline shot I've ever had in my life.

You might find you have a teen who doesn't want to go out mixing with other children and would rather stay at home. Social anxiety can feature in up to 30% of ADHD children so if sport or joining groups is the last thing they want to do, then you need to start being creative about what they can do at home. Perhaps they might like to bake? Or knit, embroider or sew? I went through a period of making bobble hats in my early teens and loved it. Whatever they are doing, as long as it's something that excites and interests them, you're onto a winner.

Now for the dangerous bit, where you haven't managed to find something to stimulate your teenager. This is when it gets a bit too risky. If they aren't getting their adrenaline from something good, the only other option is something bad. That might mean that they start drinking at an early age or taking recreational party drugs.

It's massively important you talk to them about this even if you don't think they're doing it. Their brain is naturally looking for excitement and if somebody offers them something at a party, they are going to find it very difficult to say no. So explain to them that their brain needs adrenaline and excitement and when somebody offers them something for the first time they need to be extremely aware that their brain is going to want to say yes.

So have the conversation with them about drugs and alcohol very early. They need to know that this is the 'not so good way of getting adrenaline' and is going to damage their young bodies and in the worst-case scenario bring on some sort of addiction.

Don't hold back with your teens about this stuff. Don't think if you don't talk about it, it won't happen. It's the complete opposite. The more you talk to them about it, the more open you are with them about it, the more you accept they are going to get offered alcohol and drugs – and it's THEIR CHOICE whether they want to indulge in what is going to get them into trouble with the police and be unhealthy for them – the best chance you have of them saying no. You can't be with them every single minute of every day and they know that. But you care about them and ultimately that's not what you want for them.

That's the message they need to hear – that you care about them and their bodies; and that they stay healthy and well and able to choose what they do in life rather than being addicted to some horrible drug, even cigarettes or alcohol; it just never ends up in a good place. They need to know this. Not in a judgmental way. In a very open, friendly, honest and 'you have all the choices' way.

But don't keep this subject hidden in the hope that it won't appear. If it's discussed openly, when it happens with a bit of luck they will tell you.

I used to have frequent talks with my ADHD niece, when she was just starting senior school, around drugs and what she might be offered. She was very keen to tell me that she wasn't stupid and she didn't want to go down that road and, touch wood, I don't think she ever did. But we were all very honest with her and said that it was something that was happening at her school, she would be offered all kinds of things and it was her choice whether she wanted to get addicted to something horrible and not know what she was putting into her body OR whether she wanted to stay in charge of HER body.

Remember ADHD people want to be in charge, so if you word it like this – that by saying no to any rubbish people offer you, you are staying in charge of what goes into your body – that is likely to appeal to an ADHD teenager's brain.

Other risk-taking activities girls often get into at a very young age are: dressing up much older than they actually are, wearing the shortest skirts and the lowest tops, smoking (because they think it makes them look cool) and enjoying pushing boundaries.

Obviously, the more you tell them not to do this, the more they are going to want to do it, so it's a difficult balance and yet another example of them wanting to risk-take and thrill-seek. The best way round this is not to criticise their choice of clothing, but to praise them where they wear something that is more flattering and less risky to be seen out in.

And watch out for teens who will do literally anything to bring some excitement into their life. I know of one teen who purposefully said something offensive to a police officer purely to challenge the officer arresting him. What followed was a chase over garden fences and back garden walls, with the teen finally appearing covered in grass and mud stains but with a smile as big as a Cheshire cat, having loved every minute of the chase.

Top Take-Aways

Accept that risk-taking and thrill-seeking needs to be managed. Your teen will want to feel in control, but you can introduce them to different activities and suggest taster sessions of things they might not have thought of.

Don't Bother …

Forcing them to carry on with any activity they have decided they don't like. Allow them to stop and try something else. Once an ADHD person's mind is made up, it very rarely changes.

DAMAGE LIMITATION TARGETS:

23
NOT THINKING OF THE CONSEQUENCES – IT'LL STRETCH YOUR IMAGINATION, BUT IT'S TRUE

I think this is probably the trait that neurotypical people find most difficult to understand. Even I didn't realise how severe it was until I was in my mid 50s. Very quick story of mine which will hopefully show how severe this trait is.

I had taken ADHD stimulant medication for the first time. I walked into my office and threw a set of keys down on a small side table. They landed near the edge. I looked at the keys and thought 'don't leave them there, because if they fall down the back you won't know where they've gone.'

And then I stood absolutely rooted to the spot. I could feel the hairs going up and down my back and I was in absolute shock. Because I realised for the first time in my entire life I had just thought of the consequence of something. And for the whole previous fifty-five years I had NOT KNOWN that I had never been thinking of the consequences – of ANYTHING. I can't begin to tell you how much this stunned me. I can still vividly remember that moment and how utterly shocked I was.

So if your child is not on ADHD medication please take it from me that they will not be thinking of the consequence of literally anything they say or do. It is part of our ADHD brain wiring – our brain just isn't interested in consequences! We're all about impulsivity and doing things straight away and not thinking about the consequence of anything.

There is rarely a time when this is a good idea, and it can get us into some truly dreadful situations. I can't begin to tell you how much trouble it can get teenagers into. But let's have a go! And I've some cracking examples from previous teenage clients.

The first thing I recommend is you explain this trait to your teen as soon as they are old enough. They need to know their brain does not think of any consequence, so stopping before they take action or speak is a very good idea – if they can manage it.

Sometimes their impulsivity will get the better of them and it's just not an option, but if there is ever a chance to stop and think before they do or say anything, it's a very good idea. Get that into their brain as young as you possibly can because it will help protect them. And keep repeating it. Keep reminding them that they won't be thinking of the consequences so to keep an eye out for when that might get them into trouble.

Here's your first cracking example. I once worked with an ADHD boy in his mid 20's in Portland prison. He was in jail for stealing his one thousandth car. Lovely boy! When I was chatting to him about this, I said, 'Be honest with me – and I won't judge you at all – but when you were just about to steal car number 1,000, did it ever enter your head that it maybe wasn't a good idea? That the consequence of you taking it might be you being back in this place?' He had been to prison numerous times, this boy.

I could see him mulling it over and he gave it some serious thought before answering, 'Honestly? No. I walked past the car, tried the door handle like I always do, it opened and the keys were sitting in the ignition. What else was I supposed to do?' He looked at me expectantly. Absolutely zero thought of the consequence, as he drove off full of excitement and adrenaline before being arrested yet again.

However, another story has a slightly happier ending. I worked with a private teen client, for 18 months, who was classic for not thinking of the consequences of anything. I drummed it into his head over and over that he had to think of the worst-case scenario at all times. It wouldn't always be the worst-case scenario, but there might be an occasion where it would be.

This boy was only about 14 when he and a friend decided to play a prank on some visitors to their school. It involved a bucket of cold water being perched on the top of a door. You know the kind of thing.

Bucket duly filled and perched, they were hiding, giggling, waiting for somebody to pass through the door when my client suddenly screeched at the other boy, 'Noooo! We've got to take it down.' His friend, perplexed, asked him why. And my boy, having had the worst-case scenario drummed into his head by me over many months, said, 'Because they might have a heart problem and the shock of it might mean they have a heart attack and die and we will get done for murder.'

Admittedly it was one of my most extreme not-thinking-of-the-consequence 'worst-case scenario' examples, but it worked. The bucket of water came down, nobody got drenched and even better nobody died.

So speaking with your teenager about worst-case scenarios is a very good idea. I always recommend you do this positively in a 'thank goodness we know your brain doesn't think of the consequence and we can make sure that doesn't get you into trouble' sort of way.

There are some ADHD kids who have so much anxiety that this trait won't get them into much trouble, but there are far more where it will. And most of them will be genuinely surprised when they find themselves in detention AGAIN for something they gave no thought to the consequences of.

Knowledge is power most definitely with this trait and the more you talk about it, the more your teenager will be aware. Medication really is the only option that is guaranteed to put the consequence thoughts into their brain. But raising their awareness around this trait and bringing it up as often as you can, without it being too obvious, will cement it into their brain that they have to think of the worst-case scenario because one day they might be unlucky enough for that to be the case.

Top Take-Aways

Remember this is how their brain works. They will not naturally think of the consequence of anything.

But you can educate them about the trait and talk positively about the benefits of trying to stop and think of the worst-case scenario before they speak or act.

Don't Bother …

Telling them off for it or lecturing them that 'they just need to think before they act' because that is just not possible.

Don't ever expect this to come naturally to them, unless they are on ADHD medication, which helps dramatically.

DAMAGE LIMITATION TARGETS:

24
HAVING A HEIGHTENED SENSE OF JUSTICE

The first night I was googling, having been told I might have ADHD, when I read this was a trait it suddenly made sense of so much of my life! ADHD people do have an incredibly heightened sense of justice.

This can leave parents quite incredulous when you recall that we also like to push boundaries and are prone to lying, especially during childhood. You would think that we wouldn't be much bothered about fairness and justice, but you would be very wrong!

Having a heightened sense of justice is very much part of ADHD. Anything unfair, unjust, or biased can absolutely inflame and incense anybody with ADHD and particularly teenagers during puberty, when traits are heightened.

This is going to potentially impact them in every area of their life. Most definitely at home, most definitely at school, most definitely with friendships and most definitely with any extracurricular activities they are involved in.

And, yet again, it can get teenagers into serious trouble. But forewarned is forearmed.

My heightened sense of justice in my teens meant I lost my house captain badge at senior school within 48 hours of being given it. During school assembly, the headmistress had spoken about a group of girls who had been badly bullying kids from the nearest infant school, even taking them into the public toilets and doing Lord alone knows what to them. Today I suspect the police would be involved. Back in those days it just meant my headmistress weeping on stage at how her girls had let her down.

These bullies were in my form room, and I let rip at them as soon as we were back from assembly. That was my heightened sense of justice, but it lost me my house captain badge which, in retrospect I think was unfair. These vile girls had terrorised little kids. I didn't physically touch any of the bullies but I did verbally make it very clear how disgusted I was with their behaviour. That's the first time I remember my heightened sense of justice actually getting me into trouble.

At home, if you want to avoid this trait impacting too much, make sure that everything is extremely fair, especially if they have brothers and sisters. Screen time, bedtime, who gets the biggest slice of pizza or cake, all of it will be very important to your ADHD child and they will feel slighted if things aren't fair. Nor will they shut up about it! At worst, it can bring on verbal or physical anger or violence because it will inflame them inside. So make sure everything is absolutely equal if you don't want a drama. If things don't get resolved fairly you risk your teen taking it into their own hands to sort – which rarely ends well!

If your child is into sports, expect this trait to show up there. I've had numerous clients tell me their teenager was sent off a rugby pitch or a football pitch after screaming at the ref 'are you blind?' Every single parent has told me that actually the teenager was right because they knew the rules inside out. But the ref didn't see it that way and they were sent off. No self-respecting ADHD teenager will be able to keep that sort of information to themselves. They will need to share it most certainly with the referee, the rest of the team, and anybody else who will listen. It's a very powerful passion, this heightened sense of justice.

Other clients I have worked with have found themselves in trouble for sticking up for others. On the whole, ADHD people cannot abide bullying and will always step in. I had a teenage client whose younger brother was beaten up and his own heightened sense of justice meant he had to seek revenge on these bullies. He was much older and the revenge he took out was much more severe. But his heightened sense of justice just couldn't let it go.

On a positive note, having a heightened sense of justice might mean your teen will become passionate about changing something for the good.

I've worked with many a teenage client who has been outraged at the way animals are treated, or our policies on refugees, and have become committed and passionate campaigners for whatever has inflamed their heightened sense of justice.

My own heightened sense of justice now is primarily reserved for the ludicrous amount of undiagnosed ADHD young offenders in prison. I campaign constantly and will shout at anybody who will listen that ADHD screening needs to happen right away throughout the criminal justice system because the young offender units and prisons are chock-a-block with undiagnosed ADHD. I think having an outlet for our heightened sense of justice is a good thing. Maybe by the time you read this book that will have happened and I will find something else to be outraged about! Schools is next on my heightened sense of justice list.

Teens need somebody to be angry at but that can most definitely be used for the good.

Top Take-Aways

Every ADHD teenager will have a heightened sense of justice, and it will show up pretty much everywhere. Educate them about it, so they understand why they get so incensed and can take positive action rather than do things that are going to put them at risk.

Don't Bother …

Telling them to calm down, to not overreact, to not turn everything into a drama, and to just let things go. It's not going to happen.

DAMAGE LIMITATION TARGETS:

25
WANTING EVERYTHING NOW – OR BETTER STILL, YESTERDAY

This trait is one of the simplest to understand. The easiest way to explain it to you is by using the example of a class A drug.

Yes, you did read that right.

Please don't think I'm any sort of drug user. In fact, many of my homeless and ex-offender clients in the past have accused me of being appallingly lacking in my knowledge of drugs. That's probably because I've never used any of them – not even weed – nor ever smoked. So despite working in and around addiction for the best part of thirty years, I'm no drugs czar.

However, I've watched enough television programmes to know what it's like for a heroin user needing their next hit.

Now think about your teenager's brain. Their brain is seeking adrenaline just like a drug user is seeking their next hit.

Can you imagine telling a heroin user that they can't have their heroin until their next birthday? Or they can't have their cocaine until they have saved their pocket money/wages up for six months? I think we know the response you would get.

For some ADHD teenagers this 'wanting everything now' is an extremely strong urge, particularly once they have set their heart on something. The minute they have decided they absolutely have to have that new sweatshirt, that tracksuit, those trainers, or that device, then their brain becomes absolutely consumed by that desire and can think of nothing else, other than getting their hands on it.

This is why your teenager will be nagging you incessantly and will not stop until you either implode or give in and throw your credit card at them telling them to 'buy the bloody thing!'.

In ADHD terms, new equals exciting. Old equals boring. And I'm afraid it never goes away. Even at my grand old age, I still get a little buzz every time I open the Amazon app and I have to rein myself in constantly from buying things, because I know by the time they arrive, even the box coming from Amazon will annoy me. Having to wrestle open the wretched thing (which I can't ever fathom thanks to my dyspraxia) and then I very probably won't want what's inside the box. It was so long ago I ordered it, I've already become bored with it. And when I say 'so long ago' that can be twenty-four hours. But a lot of thoughts go through an ADHD brain in those twenty-four hours!

It's taken me a very, very long time to get to this point though, after I'd spent most of my life wanting and buying everything NOW. For me, this has been particularly stationery, handbags, purses, diaries – of which I have at least ten a year, probably more and at its worst cars and houses. As soon as I have decided I want something, very little stands in the way of me having it. In fact, the only thing when I was younger was lack of money. This is where you have to be careful with your teenager, because their desire for wanting something now can very easily lead to them pinching it rather than waiting for it.

There are a few tried and tested ways I have used with clients that really help with this 'wanting everything now' conundrum. One way is to allow your teenager to put everything they want in an Amazon basket throughout the week and then have one day where you will sit down with them and decide what they actually do still want and what they don't. This works just as well for adults.

By the time people go back to the basket I can almost guarantee that 9/10 of what they've put in there, they don't even want anymore. So it's a very good way of satisfying the brain by putting it into an Amazon basket or an eBay basket or any other website basket – but only purchasing one day a week. One client used to do this every week, buying things on a Thursday so that they arrived on the Friday and he had everything new for the weekend. It's certainly worth trying if your teenager wants everything now and uses any sort of online shopping account.

When your children were younger, you could probably get away with buying cheap trainers and tracksuits but when they near their teens, beware. Two words that put the fear of God into most parents of ADHD teenagers: Designer Label.

Suddenly nothing is worth having unless it has a designer name attached to it. If it's not a Ralphie or Nike or Adidas, it's rubbish. Not only do teenagers want things now, but it has to be the right things, giving them the desired image and allowing them to keep up with their friends.

My very best advice to deal with this wanting things now situation is to get your teenager working as soon as possible. You might prefer that's in the house and you start them gardening, washing cars or doing other household chores to earn money. Others prefer to get a job in a shop or a café, or anywhere else where they can legally work in their early teens.

As soon as they are starting to earn money and know that they can use it to buy things, your life is going to get a lot easier. There are tons of other reasons why it's good to get your child working as soon as possible and this will crop up in other chapters. But if they want things now, and it has to be the right designer label, then let them start working and earn the money to pay for it themselves.

They will appreciate things a lot more, look after them better and value them more. I've seen parents who buy teenagers everything they want. The teenagers don't do a jot of work for it and it doesn't do them any favours. Instead it turns teenagers into young adults who expect everything to be given to them for nothing and they don't feel they have any sort of responsibility for earning money and providing for themselves.

Bargaining also works well with ADHD brains. So if your teen is beyond desperate to get their hands on something new you can use this to your advantage. By offering to contribute 50% or even 100% in return for whatever needs to change i.e., getting up in the morning, doing homework with no nagging, not kicking the furniture for a set period of time e.g. a month, you will help them reach their goal quicker. ADHD brains like to bargain, so as long as the odds appear to be in their favour, your chances are good of them taking up your offer.

I know of parents who think that children shouldn't work and instead focus purely on their education. Personally I strongly think all adolescents should start to earn some money from their early teens onwards. It gives them a much better understanding of how much things cost, and if they want things now they know that they have to work to earn the money to get them. This in turn really does give you a much better, well-rounded and confident adult, who knows that they have to work to earn money themselves to have what they want.

Top Take-Aways

Wanting everything now is an ADHD trait, but it is one you can manage. Earning their own money is the best way for them to realise they can have what they want as long as they work hard and save up.

Don't Bother ...

Asking an ADHD teenager to wait several months for something you know they want now. Instead find other ways of them working or earning money so they can have it sooner.

DAMAGE LIMITATION TARGETS:

26
WHEN THEY SUDDENLY KNOW BEST ABOUT EVERYTHING, INTERRUPT CONSTANTLY, AND TAKE OVER WHATEVER YOU'RE DOING

These are actually three separate ADHD traits, but they all interweave so it seems sensible to explain the connection between all of them in one go. But firstly we will break it down, so you know exactly what we're talking about.

Always knowing best – I don't know which god or scientist put this into our brain, but he or she didn't do us any favours for sure. ADHD people have this strong feeling that they know best about everything. I find this quite incredulous. For example, I have dyscalculia and am absolutely abysmal at maths, my ADHD inattention is appalling and I'm so dyspraxic I annoy myself on a daily basis, yet I still have a very strong feeling that I know best! And your teenager will be the same. Not only the same as me but almost definitely heightened because of puberty. So the feeling they know best will permeate every area of their life.

While your 7-year-old might have been quite happy to listen to you, hang on your every word and believe everything you told them, come thirteen they might decide that everything that comes out of your mouth is utter rubbish and they aren't listening to a word of it.

For some parents, this literally happens overnight. I've spoken to many client parents who have said, 'it was literally like a light switch. For eight years she did as she was told, was as good as gold but yesterday I was trying to help her with her homework when she told me, I was "full of shit" and "she knows what she's doing so leave her alone".'

Next, interrupting constantly can be for one of two main reasons. The first is that our poor short-term memory means we often forget what we want to say by the time somebody has finished waffling on during a particularly long monologue. So we will interrupt before we forget what we need to say.

But interrupting can also be to do with this trait we are talking about here. We will interrupt when we think we know better about something. When somebody is talking twaddle as far as we are concerned, we will interrupt to stop this nonsense as soon as possible and give them our opinion of what we KNOW is correct because we KNOW we are always right.

And then the final of the trilogy. Taking over what others are doing. Sometimes we are so frustrated at how slow somebody is or how they are going the long-winded way around doing something that we will just plough in, take over and do it in what we know is the right way. Because we know best!

I have heard some classics in my therapy room over the years. One father client told me how his 11-year-old son had decided he knew more about computers than his dad, who had been an IT consultant for the last thirty years.

When I was in my early teens I used to swagger up to the blackboard in classes and, with obvious delight, correct the teacher's spelling mistakes. Always with a great flourish, and expecting praise for my superior knowledge. I don't think I ever got it. I think I was just told to sit back down and shut up. But my strong 'always knowing best' trait meant I had to get up and correct those mistakes.

These ADHD traits are going to cause huge problems with siblings and friendships. You can imagine a group of friends where one always thinks they know best, will interrupt anybody suggesting anything else and take over when they think they can do things better. They are not going to be the kind of friend a lot of people want.

I can truthfully tell you that these traits have lost me friends as an adult. I don't remember it losing me friends when I was younger. It probably did. But it has definitely lost me friends as an adult. It's something I find very difficult to rein in.

Knowing best is also going to cause problems with teachers and after-school activities. I remember vividly being thrown out of the Girl Guides when I had only been there a year. The Guide leader (who really was a nice but wet wimp) admitted to my mother that I had taken over running the group 'and to be truthful, she does do it well, but I can't have a 12-year-old running my Guide pack'. This is our trouble! We're often pretty good at doing things and we don't have much time or patience for people who aren't!

At its worst – and I do include myself in this – we go through a patch in our teens of thinking everybody else is stupid, thick, slow, gormless and nowhere near as enlightened and intelligent as we are. It means we won't back down in arguments, because our brain genuinely does think it knows best. And we will always, ALWAYS want to have the last word.

So my advice to you is not to exhaust yourself fighting with an ADHD teenager who thinks they know best, because nothing you say is going to change their mind.

If you are having trouble with their teachers around them always knowing best, it might be wise to explain this trait to all teachers they come into contact with; it really is the way their brain is wired and is going to be very obvious and uncontrolled during those teenage years.

It's best not to challenge or try to correct an ADHD child constantly because that will just infuriate and incense them. It's best to just accept it as their opinion, and not engage in fighting talk.

The only time it's worth battling your teenager is if they think they know best about anything illegal, dangerous or where they will put themselves at risk of harm. So a child who thinks they know best about nicking their dad's car because 'they are sixteen, and quite old enough to drive now thank you very much', yes they do need challenging.

But never underestimate how strong this trait can be. I've met mothers desperately trying to convince ADHD teenagers that dealing drugs is a very stupid and dangerous idea but their bull-headed teens are sure they won't get caught because … insert any number of crazy reasons. They've tried everything to get through to them from therapy, to bribery, to threats, and nothing shakes that teen from thinking they know best. It's a dangerous trait but the best combo that I know to get on top of it is:

1. Medication

2. ADHD coaching

3. Introducing them to ex-offenders who tell them the truth about what awaits them if they carry on. If your teen needs this, get in touch with us – we have plenty of reformed offenders who will hit them with the hard truths prison has in store for them.

Top Take-Aways

Your teenager isn't choosing to act and feel better than other people. It literally is the way their brain is wired. And until they learn what is socially acceptable in their late teens/early 20s, it's best to just accept this is going to be heightened during their teenage years.

And know that some of their knowing best, interrupting you to correct you and taking over when they think they can do something better, is just part of their condition, not a character flaw.

Don't Bother …

Arguing the toss with them to put them right. Learn to use the word 'okay', even when they are talking tripe. They will always want the last word and you're just going to waste your energy getting them to think any other way. Unless it's illegal or criminal thinking, in which case you do need to leap on it, and quickly.

DAMAGE LIMITATION TARGETS:

27
SIBLING RIVALRY – WHAT BROTHERS AND SISTERS NEED TO KNOW!

If your ADHD child has any brothers or sisters, the very first thing I recommend is that they know your ADHD child has the condition. It doesn't do anybody any favours keeping people in the dark. I have seen families do this and it doesn't work. It's much better that all children in the family know who has ADHD and who doesn't and – age appropriately – learn as much about the condition as will help them and family dynamics.

Always talk to siblings in confidence about their brother or sister's ADHD and explain how their different brain wiring makes them at times speak, act and behave in a different manner. This in no way means they are better or worse than the neurotypical sibling, but it does mean they are different. Your children need to learn this from as young an age as possible. I would suggest probably 7 or 8 is about ideal, and most definitely by the time they reach their teens.

Depending on their maturity and level of understanding, knowing the other child has a different brain wiring and therefore sees and experiences the world differently will always be beneficial, and explain a lot.

Always watch out for the non-ADHD children in the family feeling left out and not as special as the ADHD child. After all, the ADHD teen gets days off for trips to the psychiatrist, misses classes at school to see an ADHD therapist, has access to fiddle toys and wobble seats, time-out cards and all sorts of other treats that the neurotypical child will feel they are missing out on. So it's hugely important you keep things equal, and if the ADHD child has had a day off school for a psychiatrist appointment, then that weekend the neurotypical child gets a day out with either Mum or Dad and made to feel special.

It's not unusual of course for all the siblings to have ADHD, and that can include more than one ADHD type. I grew up in a household with one Inattentive ADHD younger brother, one we're not sure about, and me with my Combined ADHD. You have to feel a bit sorry for my mother dealing with that concoction, and trying to keep us all acting and behaving exactly the same was a lost cause – but she tried!

If all your children are ADHD – and I have seen families with three or four ADHD children – don't think they're all going to be the same. They will all have different severities, possibly different types of ADHD, different coexisting conditions and different personalities. There will be traits that float consistently between them, but they will all need different handling. The clashes will be stronger, the heightened sense of justice issues between them all will be fought to the death, and your main job will be making sure that everything is seen to be fair. As soon as it's not, Rejection Sensitive Dysphoria will hit the one who is feeling left out, and that might manifest in some sort of emotional outburst or even a meltdown. Fairness in everything is key to harmonious households!

The most damaging thing you can do is have an obvious favourite. I grew up in a house with an obvious favourite and it wasn't me. That leads to chronically low self-esteem. When you spend the first eighteen years of your life living in an environment where you don't feel as good as one of your siblings, it does dreadful things to your self-worth. It also turns you into a people pleaser, because you are constantly seeking approval. Only now, many decades later, do I understand all the reasons for this. So if you do have a favourite then I strongly urge you to hide it well – very well! ADHD kids have low self-esteem as it is and the very last thing you want is them feeling not good enough compared to any other siblings. Equally, if the ADHD child is your favourite, it won't do the neurotypical child any good feeling or knowing that.

Encourage siblings to have their own outside interests. Even if this does mean you running a taxi service as you drop one after the next to different activities. It will benefit them to spend time with other teens who share their passions.

And if any of your children, especially your ADHD children, seem to want to spend an inordinate amount of time in their bedrooms, let them. Especially during their teenage years. I remember being desperate to escape to my bedroom and away from the noise of two younger brothers and a demanding mother. I used to shut my bedroom door and feel cocooned in my world of peace. A lot of parents I've worked with worry about the amount of time ADHD teenagers spend in their bedrooms. I really wouldn't. As long as they are coming out for their dinner and having some sort of interaction with others in the house for the time it takes for them to wolf down their tea, leaving them to the solitude of their bedrooms is a very good idea. Where possible let them have their own bedrooms. I know sometimes this isn't financially viable, but an ADHD child will have so much going on in their head, be coping with so much at school, that letting them have their own space is ideal if you possibly can.

If you have a reward system in place for your ADHD child, always make sure you have something similar for all the other children in the household. Your ADHD teenager's rewards might be behavioural based, and you might not have any of these behavioural issues with the other children. So I strongly suggest instead you use reward systems for them to meet their goals. These goals might be to spend five hours a week on piano practice; to do all their homework during the week, giving them weekends free; or to visit their nan at least twice a week. Then if they meet their goals they too get rewards.

Encourage a culture of understanding and accepting difference. It's never too young to learn this. But it's a lot easier said than done, I know.

And, where possible, ask your neurotypical kids not to react when an ADHD sibling has any sort of rant or meltdown. These will be much shorter lived if nobody is taking the mickey or mimicking behaviours. Ask the neurotypical siblings to steer clear and leave the ADHD teen to get whatever it is out of their system without onlookers.

Top Take-Aways

Fairness is key. Allow siblings to have their own interests, their own space and as much as possible their own autonomy. They won't like being told what to do – especially the ADHD ones!

Don't Bother ...

Forcing your ADHD teenager to do things they really don't want to do just because their brother or sister is doing it. Dad might want to sit and watch the tennis finals with all his kids, but if his ADHD son would rather lock himself in his bedroom, then allow him. Dad will enjoy the tennis much more without a grumpy, bored teenager fidgeting, fiddling or doodling next to him.

Expecting all your children to behave the same because they are all being brought up in the same house. If some have ADHD and some don't, there are going to be huge differences in their needs. This is okay. This is not a failure to get all the kids to behave the same. This is understanding the different brain wirings and making sure those are taken into account.

DAMAGE LIMITATION TARGETS:

28
ANGER, VIOLENCE AND MELTDOWNS.
TAKE COVER – ANGRY TEEN ALERT

It always sounds like a get-out when you say 'this can be anything from minor to major', but there really is no norm when it comes to anger, violence and meltdowns in ADHD teenagers. All I can say is some of these dysregulated emotions are likely to feature, but on what scale will very much depend on your own adolescent!

I'm going to tell you about some of the most extreme cases because it will be helpful if you are dealing with lesser anger in your own teenager. And the parents dealing with the more severe need to know a) that they are not alone and b) the best way other parents have found to manage these episodes.

As a teenager, I think I was probably on the lesser end of the scale. Put it this way, I have never been in a fight, never punched or slapped anybody and wasn't prone to temper tantrums or meltdowns primarily because my mother wouldn't have allowed it. She was very much of the 'you behave yourself, stop making a fuss, stop drawing attention to yourself and don't be such a drama queen' mothering style. No 'gentle parenting' in our house so I shut up and seethed internally.

But was I an angry teen? Yes most definitely. Probably permanently frustrated and irritated more than angry, but it did sometimes tip over into anger. It didn't ever tip over into violence mainly because of that very strong-willed mother at home who I knew would verbally annihilate me if I ever did anything so silly as to punch anybody. I don't ever actually remember wanting to punch anybody either, but I do remember a phenomenal amount of irritation and frustration about pretty much everything and everyone.

Only a handful of people didn't drive me nuts. One was my dad, who I absolutely know is where I inherited my ADHD from, and one was my nan who I adored. And then there were my aunt, uncle and cousins; I spent many years wishing I'd been born into that family instead. But everybody else? Couldn't stand them.

Having worked with hundreds of ADHD teenagers now, I find I wasn't alone. I'm 100% convinced this is to do with puberty, and I firmly believe all teenagers become short-tempered, frustrated and arsey almost overnight as the hormones kick in. It's well documented that ADHD traits are heightened at the beginning and end of puberty, but those actual years of puberty can be very different. Puberty started for me at twelve and ended at about sixteen or seventeen. Some parents have the deep joy of puberty arriving unexpectedly early from about the age of 9. I've met numerous parents with 9-year-old children who have changed overnight once those hormones start rattling around their body.

Every teenager, ADHD or not, goes through a lot during their teens. Not only their body changing, but more demands on them at school, with friendships, first relationships, the pressure of social media – which didn't exist when I was a teen – and huge amounts of pressure when it comes to making decisions about GCSE options, colleges, universities and careers.

And at the same time as that, if they have ADHD, they are fighting to rein in their natural impulsivity, hyperactivity, distraction, and all the other dozens of traits jostling for attention. So is it any wonder that ADHD teenagers are prone to losing their temper? I think not.

So let's first go through some examples of how this anger, frustration and irritation might play out. The very obvious one, mostly for boys but also some girls, is fighting. Physical fighting. Especially with younger brothers or sisters. I remember physical fights with my brother, who was five and a half years younger than me, wrestling on the rug – and the day I stopped was the day I felt he had become stronger than me. I knew my days of coming out on top were over, so I stepped aside, as his own puberty started I suspect.

Your own teenager may start getting into physical fights from any age, but it is definitely going to ramp up when the hormones kick in. It's not going to be unusual for your children to have physical fights and, difficult as it is, I do strongly suggest you break them up as quickly as possible and move them into different rooms. I've known of serious damage done by kids having what started as a tumble on the carpet and became somebody smashing their head open on a stone fireplace hearth.

As well as fighting with siblings and friends, your teenager might decide that inanimate objects are so annoying, or they have so much pent-up anger inside them, that the only way to get it out is to kick, punch or shove something: ANYTHING OR ANYONE. This is why my main advice is to keep you and other family members well out of the way. We are looking at damage limitation here!

Any of this is pretty standard behaviour for ADHD teens ~

- Shouting, kicking, punching, slapping or biting brothers, sisters or parents

- Kicking furniture, particularly in their bedroom. For example, wardrobes, beds, chests of drawers, mirrors and televisions

- Smashing up phones, laptops, tablets, or any device that is frustrating them – possibly because it's stopped working or they are losing at something

- Going out of the house and kicking something they find along the way. This could be neighbours' plant pots, wheelie bins, fences, cars or literally anything they walk past

Hopefully they will manage to find enough innocent things to kick that won't get them into trouble with the law. But this is an early way that young teenagers find themselves in bother with the police because kicking the wrong thing can suddenly be labelled 'criminal damage'. I've met dozens of teenagers who have been arrested for criminal damage because they kicked the wrong thing at the wrong time and somebody reported them.

If their anger is directed at you, then although it might not seem like it, this is much safer. I've met many an ADHD teenager who has kicked and punched their mother. They are normally sensible enough to know that kicking or punching their father, if they have one in their life, is not such a good idea because Dad is stronger than them. But mothers I have met have come in for a terrible beating. A lot of them have been bruised, cut and deeply upset when their child has been violent against them. Understandably so.

Most teenagers use violence when they don't feel they are being heard or understood so I hugely recommend lots of C words at this point. No, not that one. Calmness. Coolness. Compassion and Communication are what works.

The most important thing to hold in your head is that they are the child and you are the adult. Although they might be screaming absolute nonsense at you, and you are probably itching to retaliate, try not to. It's your job to stay cool, calm and collected when they can't.

They can't because their hormonal changes and puberty are playing havoc with their emotions and their ability to regulate themselves.

There really is a cacophony of emotional dysregulation going on in their body so, while I totally understand that you may want to have a go back, it's the last thing you should do if you want this to end.

What every ADHD teenager who is having a rant, a violent outburst or kicking off wants is to be HEARD. I promise you this. They want you to listen to what they are saying. To understand why they are angry and to at the very least acknowledge it if you can't totally accept it. Because it might be completely unreasonable.

So while it might be total and utter nonsense coming out of their mouth, that's the last impression you must give. Take them seriously, listen to what they have to say, ask them what the problem is and what you can do to help. Don't do this in their face while they are still ranting. Let them get it all out. Sometimes these rants can go on for a good 10–15 minutes. But you interrupting is only going to make things worse so the main thing you need to do at first is let them get it all out. If you sit and listen intently you are far less likely to get the physical responses from them.

The physical responses arise when they are not being heard and not being listened to. So give them your undivided attention. Make it very clear you want to know what is wrong and what their opinion is and then sit and listen.

This tactic is the easiest to do as you literally need to do nothing apart from look at them and appear interested. Nod a lot and use the word 'okay' where appropriate. Let them rant and rant and rant until they can rant no more and then at that point it's time for the compassion and the communication to try to resolve matters to their satisfaction.

Don't forget, ADHD teenagers think they know best about everything and want their own way so, however unreasonable they are being, make it very clear that you will take this on board as their opinion, you will consider it and you will come back to them and have a chat about it at another time. They need to know that you are not writing off what they are saying immediately.

A lot of ADHD teens need to get their anger out physically. It can literally boil away inside them until it's released. If this is your teen, and you can see in their eyes that there is rage there needing an outlet, have something and somewhere your teen can go to do this. Best ideas I've seen work well are having a punch ball or a punch bag in a basement, garage, summer house or somewhere where the teen can't be seen beating the life out of it. I've known parents have an old mattress or sofa with tatty cushions that the ADHD rage can be taken out on with absolutely no judgment by anyone.

It can be very exhausting for an ADHD teenager to rant and get everything out, so if they want to escape to their room afterwards, let them. They will need to recover. Don't immediately insist they sit down and eat their dinner, or come out in the car with you to take their brother to Cubs. They will most likely want some time on their own to calm down and to regulate themselves again.

It's usually best to wait until the next day to have a conversation about the rant if you feel it's necessary. Asking them if they would like to talk about it is a good starting point because they might feel that everything that needs to be said has been said.

But if you have promised you will come back to them about something that maybe they thought was completely unfair, then I strongly suggest you bring it up when they are in a good mood, you are alone and when things are calm and happy in the house.

It might sound a bit extreme, but if you think of a child having an epileptic fit, you wouldn't dream of judging them for it. Your child losing their temper and having a rant is a symptom of their condition so they don't need judging for it either and they don't need telling off. But they do need understanding. Remember: behind every behaviour is a feeling and it's up to you to find out what they were feeling and what caused that meltdown.

One recurring theme in my therapy room with teenagers who have been kicking off at home is the feeling they are being micromanaged by their parents. There is nothing that irritates a teenager more than not feeling they have some autonomy and freedom. Even if this is only the right to go into their room and shut the door when they need to be on their own. Parents who are in their face all the time, trying to get them to behave are always going to irritate ADHD teenagers.

One teenager I worked with hated the fact that his mother would just barge into his room unannounced. We found a compromise in that if his door was slightly open she was welcome to walk in, but if his door was shut, then she had to knock and wait to be invited in. It's tiny changes like this that make all the difference to an ADHD teenager feeling in charge of their life, which is what they want.

Also keep an eye out for self-harm when your ADHD teen has had a major episode. Some will tell you that they can only 'release the rage' by cutting or burning themselves. This is not ideal, obviously, so finding another way for them to release all their pent-up emotions and feelings is crucial.

Top Take-Aways

This isn't a choice. Puberty and hormones will mean your teenager will have a level of irritation, frustration and potentially anger and meltdowns leading to violence. It comes with their ADHD. And always remember: this is part of the condition they didn't choose but were born with. How you manage this trait is the only choice you have. You don't have the choice of whether or not they will be angry at times during their teenage years.

Don't Bother …

Trying to turn them into a calm, serene, contented and sweet-natured teenager. Good luck with that if you try! You might be lucky, and have a teenager who is barely bothered by their puberty, and is gentle, calm and kind all the way through their teenage years. But don't hold your breath as it's very unlikely.

DAMAGE LIMITATION TARGETS:

29

FRIENDSHIPS – ALL THE PROBLEMS THEY CAN BRING AND HOW TO FIND YOUR TRIBE

This is a very big issue and I'm going to break it up into categories because there's a lot of ground to cover.

Firstly, this is such a common reason parents bring their children for ADHD therapy. Lack of friendships or losing friendships and becoming isolated and lonely is a very common theme. So let's dig deeper into this and find out why.

WHY MIGHT ADHD TEENS STRUGGLE TO MAKE FRIENDS?

Let's start off with the ADHD adolescents who have social anxiety – that's up to 30% of them. These kids will often struggle to integrate and will usually be uncomfortable in the company of others. Some of these teens are genuinely happier on their own and can occupy themselves at break time quite easily without any interaction at all.

It's when they are forced to join in with others that they become uncomfortable. Some find it absolutely impossible and shouldn't be forced to 'get along with the others' if they really don't want to.

Then there are the children with social anxiety who find one friend, often somebody with either ADHD or ASD, or some other sort of different brain wiring, who will become their one and only best friend, and that suits them both just fine.

However, if your child does want to make friends and is struggling to, there could be all sorts of ADHD traits coming into play here. ADHD teens can be very excitable, hyperactive, lively and in your face. This can be too much for some neurotypical kids who will gradually exclude the noisy, hyper one, and it's very painful for the ADHD child to be pushed out when they are usually doing their very best to fit in.

Being left out or excluded is crippling for ADHD teens due to the Rejection Sensitive Dysphoria element of their condition. Being left out of events in or outside of school by people they considered friends will be horrifically painful to deal with. Don't underestimate how dejected, rejected and hurt they will feel. It can be all-consuming and attack their already low self-esteem. It can make their life hell, 24/7, as not fitting in and having no friends can be seen as 'weak' at school.

Other ADHD traits that get in the way of friendships are impulsivity, wanting everything our own way, needing to feel in charge, feeling we know best and not having patience for people who are slower on the uptake or less skilled at an activity. The ADHD child won't be able to cover up their annoyance or frustration as well as others and this can lose them friendships very easily. It can also see them getting thrown out of team activities for not showing sportsmanship.

WHY THEY MAY FLIT FROM ONE FRIENDSHIP GROUP TO ANOTHER

This is most often because of boredom. Once an ADHD teen knows somebody inside out and has played every game with them and talked about every subject under the sun, their brain will naturally seek out someone new and therefore more exciting. Numerous client parents have told me that teachers have informed them they are worried about their child 'because they seem to flit from group to group'. This really is absolutely nothing to worry about. It's just your child seeking adrenaline and a dopamine hit from meeting new people, listening to different stories, hearing fresh jokes and doing alternative activities with a new group.

WHY THEY MAY LOSE VERY GOOD FRIENDS

Sadly I can speak from personal experience here. Even as an adult. Often ADHD people say things without thinking. Remember, we don't think of the consequence, so words can come out of our mouths before we've thought it through even for a second.

I'll give you one classic example of mine that lost me a friend of 25 years. She had been moaning about the price of cat food. The following week her cat died, and she put a post up about it on Facebook. I quipped 'at least it will save the cost of the cat food'. She hasn't spoken to me since.

ADHD teenagers can say quite harsh things and then five minutes later have completely forgotten they've said it. But the neurotypical person won't have forgotten and they won't move on quite so quickly. And as ADHD people are known for not sugar-coating things and for 'saying it as it is' this can get us into all sorts of trouble with friendships.

ADHD teenagers can also be very obsessive and fixated with their friends. Fixation is a trait of ADHD so if your teenager finds one friend who they absolutely worship and adore, they may become very obsessive, territorial and protective of that friend and become VERY upset when this friend has anything to do with anybody else.

Obsessions and fixations are most definitely part of how the ADHD brain works and for a lot of teenagers this is just too much. They may well want to be friends with your ADHD daughter, but they may also want other friends and this may not sit so well with your own teen. It won't only be obsession and fixation – it will also be their low self-esteem. Worrying that their friend is going to go off with this new friend and they will be left behind. Alone. That constant worry and anxiety about hanging onto friendships can actually be too much for others, who then pull away.

WHEN FRIENDS CAN EQUAL DANGER

I've seen this dozens of times so please be wary of it. When you are an ADHD teen, anybody older means they are more interesting to you and therefore more exciting. These older teens will often utilise a younger teen to do things they don't want to get caught for themselves.

It's very easy for younger teens to be flattered by older teenagers' attention but more often than not this is because they want something from the younger teen and in my experience that is nearly always dodgy.

So if your 13-year-old suddenly tells you they are best mates with a 16-year-old, most definitely find out a lot more about this 16-year-old. If it turns out they are a genuinely nice kid and have shared interests with your 13-year-old then fine, but I would always be extremely wary of anybody more than a year older than your own teenager and what their motives are. I've seen it so many times when older teenagers get younger ADHD teenagers into trouble, especially as ADHD adolescents have low self-worth so they are likely to be drawn to anybody showing them attention.

Worst-case scenario is older teenagers are getting your young teenager involved in drugs. It's a well-known fact that older teenagers use younger ones to run 'county lines' drug deals and I've known boys as young as 14 get caught up in this and end up in prison. So most definitely get your detective hat on and find out exactly who your teenager is mixing with. In this instance, it's much better that you are a nosy, overbearing parent rather than your teenager ends up arrested for anything to do with drugs.

BUT THE GOOD NEWS! WHERE THEY WILL ALWAYS FIND FRIENDS

I have very good news for you. Although your ADHD son or daughter may struggle to find friends at school, there is one place they are absolutely guaranteed to find friends, often lifelong friends. And that is with people who share the same interests as them.

I'm a classic example. I didn't hang onto any friends from school, but from the moment I joined an amateur dramatic society and found other people who loved acting as much as me, I found friends who have lasted for life. Some of these friends I've now had for forty years. And I still adore all of them.

So if your child is struggling to make or keep friends at school I strongly recommend you encourage them to join at least one after-school club where they will meet people with a shared interest. It doesn't matter what that shared interest is. It could be helping at the local donkey sanctuary, playing tennis, an after-school chess club, tae kwon do or anything your child shows the faintest bit of interest in.

Encourage them to join a local club or support group where they will meet others with the same interests and hey presto! friendships will form. I've seen this numerous times with dozens of clients as well. Boys who have not been able to make or keep any friends at school, but as soon as they join a boxing club, a football club or a rugby club, they are suddenly surrounded by people with the same passions. They make very quick connections that last.

This has been the answer to friendship problems so many times I can 100% promise you it's worth pursuing if your child is really feeling the lack of good solid friendships.

Top Take-Aways

Take any friendship issues seriously because they can absolutely destroy your teenager's life if things aren't going well. Remember all the ADHD traits that might be impacting friendships. Be ready to listen to your teen and gently remind them of the traits that might be impacting any problems they are going through with friends.

Don't Bother …

Forcing your child to be friends with people they aren't interested in. You might be great mates with your next door neighbour, but your daughter might think her daughter is the most boring person on the planet. Friends need to stimulate an ADHD teen's brain, so there's no point forcing friendships on them.

Don't dismiss it as irrelevant if your early teen is finding older, more exciting teens appealing. It's natural, but something you need to be wary of because older teenagers may well utilise yours for risky activities.

DAMAGE LIMITATION TARGETS:

30
BULLYING – WHY IT HAPPENS AND WHAT TO DO WHEN THEY ARE BULLIED, OR ARE THE BULLY

It's not uncommon for ADHD kids to be bullied for one plain and simple reason: they are different. And we all know that at school being different is the very worst thing you want to be because it makes you a target for bullies.

I had fitted in beautifully at junior school, but come my hideous secondary school experience, where I was at the wrong school due to that spectacular failure of my 12-plus, I felt I was amongst aliens.

I was lumped in with girls who thought slashing their wrists and getting pregnant at 13 was the way to go. I was horrified, having come from a quite upmarket middle school. I must've stood out like a sore thumb. Wearing my uniform neatly, never skipping school, always doing my homework, enthusiastically partaking in all the sports and drama activities, never smoking and not going near a boy until I was at least 17. So of course, the inevitable happened. I was bullied. Not at first. I think it probably started around the age of 13 or 14 but it made my life absolute hell.

I begged and pleaded with my mother to change school, but she wouldn't because the alternative one meant a much longer drive and she had my two younger brothers to get to school in the mornings. I won't say I was ever suicidal over it, but my life was utterly miserable being bullied by only a very small group of girls, but girls who constantly called me names, screamed abuse in my face, one even pulled me backwards by my hair off a very high stool in science, and my life really was unbearable for a good year or two at senior school. It was so bad the headmistress let me leave five minutes early to get away from the school before the bullies could get to me.

So please have a LOT of understanding if your teenager tells you they are being bullied. It really can be a horrifically scary and traumatic time for them.

I don't think enough was done when I was being bullied. My mother should have gone to the school and spoken to them seriously, and now I would advise that you go and speak to the SENCO. They have to know if an ADHD child is being bullied persistently and something needs to be done about it. Don't let your child suffer in silence like I had to for probably 18 months. Always do this in conjunction with your teen though. Don't ever do anything behind their back. And always make decisions together about what is going to happen next. It gives them some control over the situation and when you are being bullied you feel very out of control.

Most importantly, your child needs to know that you are on their side, that this isn't acceptable, and that it isn't anything they have done. If they are being bullied because of their ADHD or their autism or any of the coexisting conditions, then explain to them that this shows ignorance, lack of tolerance and understanding from the bully and is in no way a reflection on or anything to do with them. If they know that you are completely and utterly on their side and prepared to do anything – in conjunction with them – to change this situation, that will give them strength during the day at school. And boy, will they need strength just to keep going in every day, not knowing what they are going to face.

You need to do everything in your power to build up your teenager's self-esteem, and it's a good tactic to arm them with some verbal responses for when the bullying next happens.

Obviously retaliating physically is never to be recommended and entering into tit-for-tat verbal fights isn't going to get them anywhere either. It will just prolong the episode. So I recommend you collaboratively come up with a stock phrase that they like and agree with and can use every time the bullies attack. Then don't waver from this so the bullies know they are only ever going to get one response out of them. It needs to be something along the lines of:

'It's your choice if you carry on, but if you do, be prepared for me to report this to the head teacher now, my parents after school and if necessary the police. You've been warned'.

IF YOUR TEEN IS THE BULLY

In my experience, this is much less likely, but it does happen. ADHD teenagers tend to have more compassion and care for the underdogs so they rarely become bullies but on occasions they will.

In these situations it's critical you sit down and talk to them non-judgmentally. You need to know exactly what they are doing and why. It might be because they are feeling threatened by other people and they are trying to prove that they are not 'wimps' themselves. This happens quite a lot in boys' schools but girls aren't immune to it. You need to find out what is behind this behaviour and why they feel the need to physically or verbally attack other teenagers. What is really going on? There could be so many things underlying here.

It could be that they have undiagnosed coexisting conditions and are terrified of looking weak, thick or hopeless and think the only way people will respect them is by using their fists. So it's really important you dig very deep to find out what is going on with your teen as they may have issues themselves.

On the even more rare occasions that there is no reason other than they enjoy bullying other people – and I can't begin to tell you how rare this is – you need to have a very good chat with them about the consequences of their actions. Encourage them to actually think about how the other person is feeling. Do they really want to make somebody terrified of going into school every day? How would they feel if that person self-harmed or worse still took their own life because they couldn't face going into school?

If they have brothers and sisters, ask them how they would feel if they were being bullied? Would they want their brother or sister to face the same treatment they are dishing out to others?

It's really a question of getting them to realise how devastating their actions can be, because they possibly haven't given it much thought. They are probably getting a buzz from feeling like the school cool guy who won't take any crap from anybody. But when you present them with the realities of the consequences of their actions, it should be relatively easy to get them to realise that they could impact the rest of their lives.

Don't forget, the bullying may well have been impulsive and without thinking of the consequences. It's up to you to allow them to know what these consequences would be – they need to know that even 13- and 14-year-olds can get criminal records. That's the last thing you want for them because you want them to have all the career and travel options they choose when they get older, but they need to change their behaviour now if it's not going to affect their future.

Make this conversation as un-judgmental as you possibly can. Make them know that you are on their side, but they need to change their behaviour now if it is not going to negatively impact their future. And you care very much about their future. It might be a conversation you need to have more than once, but keep having it until their behaviour changes.

Top Take-Aways

It's not unusual for ADHD kids to be bullied. It is important to do something about it as quickly as possible and always collaboratively with your teenager. Make sure they know you are on their side and together you will get this bullying stopped.

Don't Bother …

Hoping it will all just go away. In my experience it doesn't. Don't tell your teenager off for putting themselves in a situation where they have allowed themselves to get bullied or for being weak. I have known parents do this. It makes the child feel not understood at home as well as at school.

DAMAGE LIMITATION TARGETS:

31
ANXIETY – AND WHY IT'S ALMOST DEFINITELY GOING TO APPEAR IN SOME SHAPE OR OTHER

Anxiety is a pain in the neck. Or more accurately in the head. Speaking as somebody with it, who doesn't want it – it's extremely annoying, but sadly we don't have a choice.

Anxiety and depression quite simply go with ADHD. This is one of the reasons that although we say we are 'turbocharged by ADHD' and 'it's a superpower' – and I strongly believe in both those statements – we always have to remember that for so many people, me included, the elements of anxiety and depression are nearly always present to some degree in all people with ADHD.

With anxiety the first thing we need to talk about is the chronic amount of misdiagnosis, especially in girls. I don't want to slate doctors because I know they are all extremely stressed and doing their best, but the amount of teenage girls I have met who have been diagnosed with anxiety when actually they have ADHD is off the scale and wholly unacceptable.

A counsellor friend of mine had a daughter who, since the age of about 11, had been seeing CAMHS which in the UK stands for Children and Adolescent Mental Health Services. I don't know one parent who doesn't actually think it should stand for Chronic Ability to Misdiagnose & Hopeless Services. Honestly, they are that shocking. I could introduce you to a thousand incensed parents who have dealt with them.

Anyway, back to my friend's daughter who had for two or three years been seeing this shower of hopelessness and been told that she had anxiety. This went on for so long in the end I said 'This is absolutely ridiculous. Anxiety doesn't come from nowhere. I know she has a lovely mother and a lovely stepfather, a lovely home – because I've been there – and she's at a very good school so please bring her to see me'.

Within half an hour we had worked out this girl had quite severe Inattentive ADHD, which was the cause of her anxiety. I sent a very strong letter to CAMHS, followed up by a phone call when they questioned my letter. I wiped the floor with them, I was so angry that they had let this girl suffer unnecessarily for years. They invited her back in and diagnosed her with Inattentive ADHD – helped, I'm sure by my letter detailing about forty traits – and her life has changed hugely since.

So firstly, if you are reading this book, wondering if your child has ADHD and they have a lot of anxiety, this is a very big red flag for undiagnosed ADHD.

It's also a very good idea to go into your doctors if you are wondering about your teenager's issues and ask to see the doctor's notes. I was staggered when I looked at mine to see right through my late teens, 20s and 30s my chronic sleep problems had been logged as 'anxiety/depression'.

This is very common so if there is a repeated pattern of the doctor summarising 'anxiety/depression' that is another red flag for undiagnosed ADHD.

Anxiety is very often the first clue in girls that they have ADHD. Because often they manage their emotions better than boys so aren't punching anybody or kicking anything, but could be riddled with unseen anxiety inside. So if your teenager isn't showing any of the Hyperactive signs, but has anxiety around a lot of things, it's very well worth digging deeper to see if there are any more ADHD traits.

Social anxiety is something that is thought to affect 30% of ADHD adolescents. Working with so many teenagers I have seen what I believe are the main two ways it presents.

The most common is not being able to stand crowds or groups of people. I've met numerous ADHD teenagers who cannot go on public transport, cannot even stand on a train platform because there are too many people, cannot manage big concerts, football stadiums, huge shopping centres and crowds of any kind. These teenagers will very happily sit and talk to you one-to-one and can very often talk your ear off with no sign of anxiety at all. But put them in any of these big environments and they are an anxious mess, desperate to escape. This is by far and away the more common version of social anxiety in my experience of ADHD teens.

There is, however, another presentation which is far less common. These teenagers actually don't mind big, noisy environments because they can lose themselves and be inconspicuous. What they hate is being trapped with one person where they are expected to talk. This gives them anxiety. A lot of them just don't know how to conduct themselves and are terrified of small talk. So they would actually rather hide in a big crowd.

School anxiety is something else that may well appear. There could be a myriad of reasons for this, and very often it's caused by an undiagnosed ADHD coexisting condition or even more than one. If your child has dyslexia, dyscalculia or the even more crippling dysgraphia, but these have not yet been identified, your teen will be anxious about being seen as stupid and told off at school and may develop chronic anxiety about going in.

Even sitting in classrooms of thirty is too much to bear for some teenagers with social anxiety. When I was working in the young offender units I used to see some of the ADHD boys locked in a grassy area box, jumping up and down with hyperactivity, and when I asked them why they were in there, it was because they couldn't be in the classroom because of their social anxiety. Of course, the prison service with its chronic lack of understanding of ADHD, didn't realise it was social anxiety connected to ADHD, and if they had only medicated them they might have had some hope of them sitting in the classroom.

Something else to be aware of is what your teenager does to cope with their anxiety. I have had teenage clients who have used alcohol to summon up the courage to go into school. Usually vodka because it doesn't smell. But this has obviously horrified parents when they have found out. Some will use cannabis to calm themselves down enough to be able to be around other people. And some will just swerve the situation altogether. Some will get so wound up with anxiety before school or events they'll actually give themselves a genuine upset stomach or be sick.

So is there anything you can do about anxiety in teenagers? Thankfully, yes. There are two things that help hugely.

The first is therapy and in particular cognitive behavioural therapy (CBT). CBT works very specifically with one issue at a time and handled properly, by a therapist who has ADHD themselves so understands how the ADHD brain works, they can give your teenager some brilliant ways of dealing with situations that make them anxious.

And the second way is ADHD medication. All anxiety is born of overthinking and ADHD medication stops overthinking. So if you have been putting off medicating your teenager, or they have been reticent about taking it, but are suffering with anxiety, do mention this as a possibility to solving the problem. It is most certainly worth a go.

Also worth knowing, if your teen isn't responding well to ADHD medication or can't be on it for any other reason, often anti-anxiety meds can be very helpful. You don't even need to see a paediatrician or psychiatrist to get anti-anxiety medication – your GP should be able to prescribe.

Top Take-Aways

Your teenager won't know anxiety is part of the condition so it's well worth explaining this to them. Some of them will find it very difficult to express their problems and won't realise they are connected to ADHD anxiety, so a lot of explaining from you as to what it is, and how it might play out, will be very helpful to them.

Don't Bother ...

Thinking this can't be crippling for some. It really can be. I've worked with clients where social anxiety has been massively impacting their education and their friendships.

And don't think it will just go away by you telling them to have more confidence and belief in themselves. This is an internal problem that can only be dealt with by medication or therapy. Or in an ideal world – both.

DAMAGE LIMITATION TARGETS:

32
DEPRESSION – VERY SCARY FOR PARENTS

If you have an undiagnosed teenager who has spent their life so far being told off for fidgeting, not ever sitting still, doodling, shaking their leg, swinging on their chair, tapping with their fingers, sucking their hair, refusing to wear certain clothes, hating labels, not liking a lot of food, feeling different, failing to focus and concentrate in class, underachieving when the teacher knows they can do better and the 1,000 other things that come with undiagnosed ADHD, it's not hard to see why they might get depressed by their teenage years.

Add in to this the hormonal changes and the fact that ADHD people are more likely to suffer with depression, you may well find yourself with a depressed teenager on your hands, and that is of course extremely worrying for parents.

Anxiety and depression can both be very much a part of ADHD but the severity differs by a huge amount. I have known ADHD adults who have been depressed since childhood and no amount of ADHD medication or antidepressants have managed to shift it. Let's hope your child isn't one of those and they are a small minority.

You may also have a teen who, like me, had what was diagnosed as 'reactive depression'. This is depression when there is a reason for it – when something external has happened to cause it. So for example, I was very depressed when my father died when I was only just 23. This is natural of course, but with ADHD depression can be much more severe because of our inability to regulate our emotions. So look out for reactive depression if there's a bereavement in the family or something else sad happens. Your ADHD child may get more low/depressed than expected.

Something to be very wary of is doctors who don't understand ADHD and will dish out antidepressants to very young teenagers. This used to make my counselling supervisor very angry. She was vastly experienced in ADHD, having brought up two sons with it, and firmly believed that no child with ADHD needs antidepressants if they are on the right ADHD medication. This was advice she encouraged me to give to a lot of clients, and I think in every case it proved to be true. Some doctors seem to be very keen to hand out antidepressants to teenagers as young as 13 or 14 when what they need to be doing is digging deeper to find out where the depression has come from. And very often that is because of undiagnosed ADHD.

I have met literally hundreds of ADHD teenagers who have been put on antidepressants when their parents know there is more going on, but are just understandably grateful for any help because they are worried sick about their teenager feeling this way.

Depression seems to affect those with Inattentive ADHD much more than those with Combined ADHD and that very small portion with purely Hyperactive/Impulsive ADHD. In my opinion there is one main reason for this, and that is feelings of under-achievement. Those with Inattentive ADHD have as many ideas, thoughts, dreams and plans as all ADHD people, but usually fail to put them into action due to chronic procrastination and lack of motivation. This leads to feelings of under-achievement and subsequently depression.

I'm generalising here, but I've seen this pattern emerge over the years. My brother is a very good example. We share the same mum but had two different dads and inherited our ADHD from each of them. My brother has been depressed his whole life and no amount of ADHD medication or antidepressants have made a jot of difference. I, however, with my Combined ADHD, only get depressed if something bad/sad actually happens. Then I do sink lower and quicker than other people into deep depression but the good news is I come out of it quicker – I'm sure this is because my brain works quicker and processes things quicker.

So if your teen seems to be permanently depressed, it's well worth investigating ADHD medication and what that can do for them first. I do know of some teenagers now who are on ADHD medication and a low dose of antidepressant and this seems to work well for them, so don't write it off as a possibility.

Top Take-Aways

Depression is part of the ADHD condition and can be particularly heightened during teenage years because of puberty. ADHD medication usually makes the world of difference, but if that's not enough, then consider therapy at the same time.

Don't Bother …

Thinking this is just your teenager being moody, stroppy and attention seeking. Depression can be absolutely debilitating for some ADHD teenagers, but with a combination of medication and therapy, the vast majority improve dramatically.

DAMAGE LIMITATION TARGETS:

33
SELF-HARM AND SUICIDE – A TOUGH SUBJECT, BUT ONE WE DO HAVE TO TALK ABOUT

Here we go. The big important stuff.

I truly do NOT want to put the fear of God into you. But knowledge is power. So deep breaths and read on.

I'll start by telling you I personally have never self-harmed or attempted suicide, nor got even close to either. So not everybody with ADHD is impacted by the higher incidences of self-harm and suicide that relate to those with ADHD in general. And I am diagnosed with moderate-to-severe ADHD. So in theory, there may well have been a risk of self-harm throughout my life.

It's important you know, but not necessarily dwell on, the fact that the rate of self-harm and suicide is higher in ADHD people, especially when not on ADHD medication. That fact is true, but the last thing I want you to do is start worrying that your own ADHD teenager is definitely at risk of self-harm or suicide attempts. Nothing could be further from the truth. Some ADHD people don't ever self-harm, nor have any suicidal thoughts at all. And let's hope your teenager is one of these.

For the parents who are dealing with adolescents where self-harm or suicide threats are featuring, this can be hugely worrying and I will try to do my very best to equip you if you find yourself in this situation.

Let's start with self-harm. When I was at counselling college, we were taught that overeating was a form of self-harm, so if we take into account the amount of cake, chocolate, sweets, ice cream and biscuits I have consumed – in some circles I would be considered a self-harmer. But apart from buying bigger clothes and avoiding the scales, that didn't really impact me.

The sort of self-harm we're talking about here is when children physically do things to their body on purpose that harm them, most often by cutting or burning their skin.

This is not unusual with ADHD teenagers and particularly relates to girls. I have worked with many ADHD teen clients who have told me that when they cut themselves, they gain an instant and satisfying release from the incessant overthinking and negative thoughts constantly going on in their head.

So my first port of call to help as always is going to be medication. ADHD medication, when it works, does some miraculous things. Probably the most helpful of which in this scenario is regulate emotions.

So if you have a teenager who is refusing medication or has come off it for any reason, then please do look at getting them back on it.

There is nothing better for levelling out their emotions, stopping overthinking and eradicating rumination.

There literally isn't one ADHD self-harming teenager I have worked with who has given any reason for doing it, other than escaping from their thoughts. Importantly, not one has told me they have done it wanting to end their life, nor because they have wanted to attract or be the centre of attention. They have literally all told me it has been when they couldn't stand the constant chattering in their head and needed to escape from their own thoughts. ADHD overthinking and rumination is at its peak in the teenage years.

So if we take a real-life example, of where a teen was being ostracised at school, didn't think any of their teachers liked them, was waiting to see if they would be charged after a recent arrest and had just split up from their girlfriend, you can imagine how this teenager was thinking and feeling. For the first time in his life, he did start to self-harm in a very minor way. But of course that worried his parents terribly.

This teenager had been on ADHD medication but had come off because of some nasty side-effects. During this episode he was seeing me as his therapist and I encouraged him to try a different ADHD medication. He wasn't keen but with gentle persistence I persuaded him to agree to try it at least. At the same time as this we spoke at length about his thoughts and feelings about all his different issues, and within a very short period of time, coinciding with him going back on the medication, the self-harm stopped.

So in no particular order my very strong advice if you find out that your ADHD adolescent is self-harming would be as follows:

1. If finances allow, book them in with an ADHD specialist counsellor who is qualified to work with children. They will be trained in self-harm and will understand how it relates in particular to ADHD. Your child will benefit from knowing they can speak to somebody in confidence about whatever is troubling them.

2. If they are not on medication, try to overcome whatever hurdles there are to get them on it. There is nothing as

powerful as ADHD medication for levelling and regulating emotions.

3. Never tell your teen off or tell them that they MUST stop self-harming. And don't make dramatic gestures like throwing out all the razorblades, locking the kitchen knife drawers and trying to restrict their access to anything sharp. All this will make them do is go to the nearest chemist and buy a razor. Instead, what you need to do is sit down and talk to them in the most non-judgmental way you possibly can. Find out what is going on for them. Why have they started to self-harm now? What has happened recently? And very importantly – what you can do to help AND how they can keep their wounds clean and uninfected.

Cutting open or burning their skin is not the only way they can self-harm. In some severe cases, I have known ADHD teenagers drink bleach and set fire to themselves. But please believe me this is extremely rare. I'm only mentioning it because if your teenager is doing this, I don't want you to feel alone and that this is only happening to your family. I promise you that's not the case.

Overdosing on pills or tablets is, along with arm cutting, probably the most common way teenagers will try to hurt themselves. We have to be very careful here because this is a condition that obviously many teens are taking pills for anyway. So having pills accessible is something that is going to be quite common.

Firstly, the risk-taking and thrill-seeking ones may well be tempted to push that boundary and take as many of their ADHD meds in one go as they possibly can. I've had one teenager show me a video on their phone, with huge delight, demonstrating how they managed to take a fortnight's worth of ADHD medication in one go. They had literally filmed themselves doing it. I was, of course, horrified and asked what the outcome was. 'I just slept extremely well for a few days' was the answer. Luckily, they had thought to tell their mother this when they finally woke up, and the pills were swiftly removed, and only given once on a daily basis from that point on.

But if you have a depressed teenager on your hands, having access to that sort of weekly or even monthly quantity of medication is not a good idea. Obviously how you manage the situation will depend very much on your teenager. Some will be very glad when you take away the responsibility of having to remember to take their medication each day. They will find it quite a relief that the medication appears on the table along with their breakfast.

Some won't like relinquishing control, and you might have a battle on your hands. If you are seriously concerned they might take too much medication, usually impulsively, it's well worth that battle of getting the medication somewhere away from their impulsive hands though. Remembering that a lot of ADHD teenagers struggle to sleep, in the early hours of the morning, when they might be lying awake with thoughts racing through their heads, having access to a large number of pills is not a good idea.

Taking just enough extra pills to get somebody to notice how bad they are feeling and how desperate they are is quite common. Of course you are going to panic if they have taken a few too many pills, but I know from experience that clients who have taken more than the recommended dose, but on a smaller scale, are usually lucky enough to either sleep it off, or in the worst-case scenario, endure a visit to A&E where sadly they usually get a telling off rather than the emotional support they need.

So just keep an eye out for teenagers having access to large quantities of any kind of pill or tablet. With their emotional dysregulation and impulsivity, heightened during puberty, keeping all family pills locked in a medicine cabinet is probably the best idea.

If the self-harm is severe and you are concerned, I strongly recommend you speak to the child's paediatrician, or if they are over 18, their psychiatrist. It's very important they know what is going on.

They may decide to adjust or change medication and they will almost definitely want you working with a professional psychotherapist or counsellor who will most probably be asked to keep in contact with the paediatrician or psychiatrist while your child goes through this.

It's also massively important you look after yourself. It's easy to forget YOU if you are concentrating very hard on your teenager's wellbeing and safety. It can be absolutely exhausting being hyper-vigilant 24/7, making sure they are safe. There are 'ADHD parenting specialists' and I strongly advise you book in with one. My own therapy company has these and they are godsends when it comes to supporting parents going through something the therapist will have had personal family experience of – but equally are trained professionally to work with.

Now, moving on to suicide.

First, let's deal with very young kids who frighten the life out of their parents by threatening to kill themselves. Sometimes from the age of 4 or 5 but more often 7 to 9. They often use it as a threat. So 'if you don't let me have another ice cream I'm going to kill myself'.

This is obviously quite shocking language and does alarm parents. But in very young children, this is nearly always impulsivity and while I never say to completely ignore comments like this, it's very likely that this is just a child being dramatic and thinking of a threat that will have the most impact and will result in them getting their own way.

I've spoken to numerous parents who are worried sick that their child is constantly saying they're going to kill themselves, or kill their parents or kill their siblings. Some of them even grab a knife from the kitchen drawer for extra impact and parents are terrified out of their wits as to what the child might do next.

On the whole, the answer to that is nothing. In nearly every case, it's a child not in control of their emotions, not getting their own way and using words for maximum impact. I say nearly always, because on that one-in-a-million occasion, you might get a teen who takes it a step further. But this is incredibly rare, so please don't take these impulsive comments seriously.

How you handle it is important, because obviously humiliating, laughing at or ridiculing your child is just going to make them angry. So my best advice in these situations is to talk very calmly to them. Ask exactly what it is they are wanting or needing and start negotiating as to how that can happen.

As children get older, into their very early teens, this is when you need to take any threats of suicide more seriously.

There will still be teens, up till around the age of 14 or 15, who will use the threat of killing themselves or killing you as a way to get their own way. Don't forget ADHD teenagers can be quite dramatic, because they are always seeking adrenaline and excitement. Therefore normal is boring. So they won't just tell you that they are miffed or cheesed off that a day out to the seaside has been cancelled and will instead tell you that they're now going to kill themselves because you have just ruined their life!

In the vast majority of cases in all teenagers, these threats are said impulsively, without thinking of the consequences, and very rarely connected to what they are actually going to do which, in this case is more than likely strop off to their bedroom, slam the door and not talk to you for the rest of the day! If, however, you have a depressed child who talks to you seriously about suicide, or you believe is so low that it is something they would contemplate, then obviously this is a very different scenario and one where you must take action.

If your teenager will agree to seeing a counsellor, then book them in immediately with an ADHD specialist one. Please note – this is not the time for an ADHD *coach*. It needs to be an ADHD counsellor who is qualified to work with teenagers. If they are 16/17-plus then an adult ADHD counsellor will be equally fine.

You do need to take this seriously at this age, because they're more likely to do something on impulse, and tragically we have heard of teenagers – very, very rarely – but ADHD teenagers who have taken their own life.

In the situations we have come across professionally the reasons for the actual suicides have been feelings of rejection and humiliation. Which is why I put so much emphasis on always building up your teen, not putting them down, being careful how you word things and keeping everything positive.

It is so easy for a teenager to take one critical comment, or a comment that they perceived as critical, and overthink and ruminate on it to the point that they just don't feel their life is worth living. This is what we have to avoid at all costs. It's critical we praise ADHD teenagers and encourage them to be positive and to channel their ADHD so they are hugely successful in the future. Their brains can so easily go in the opposite direction.

I've been working in the ADHD world for eight years since my diagnosis, and it's only in the last year that suicide has touched my life. We know of a girl who was 16, who took her own life, and one of my ex-young offenders, who I have known since he was 21, aged 30 took his own life.

It's rare, but it happens.

Top Take Aways

Self-harm and/or suicide threats may not feature in your ADHD teenager at all. But if they do, there is professional help available and you need to access it as quickly as possible.

Don't Bother …

Worrying that every idle threat is of serious concern. If your teenager is known for throwing around comments, like 'killing themselves' or 'killing the neighbours' or 'killing you' and five minutes later, not even remember they said it, it won't benefit you to pick them up on it every single time.

Remember they will still be speaking impulsively and without thinking of the consequences, especially if not on medication.

DAMAGE LIMITATION TARGETS:

34
FIRST RELATIONSHIPS ... OF THE ROMANTIC KIND AND THE ROLLERCOASTER IT CAN BE

This might have come earlier, but it's most likely by the time they get into their early teens that your adolescent's thoughts will turn to the opposite sex. (And/or, of course, for some of them, the same sex.)

Relationships are difficult for everybody to navigate, but add in all the ADHD traits and it can be a minefield.

First, let's start with crushes. It won't be unusual for your teenager to fall head over heels in love with somebody and have very strong thoughts about them – potentially without the love interest being even faintly aware. I certainly know this was the case for me. I had some incredibly strong crushes by the time I reached about 12 or 13.

I used to walk up and down outside whichever boy's house I was crazy about, itching to see him. I never did of course. He probably wasn't even in. But I remember lurking in bushes and staring up at bedroom windows longing for heaven knows what. I can so easily recall the power of those feelings and how they stayed with me 24/7. I was utterly obsessed and fixated on which ever oblivious teenager it was at the time.

I was right in the middle of a major crush on actor Richard Beckinsale at 15 when he unexpectedly died at the age of 31, which absolutely crucified me. Your teenager's emotions might also be surprisingly strong. And even if they have a crush on somebody and those feelings are not returned, like mine, it is going to bring out some surprisingly strong emotions in your own teen.

It might see them spending hours in their bedroom thinking, moping and dreaming. Even crying with the frustration of unrequited love. It might make them snappy and rude when their feelings aren't being reciprocated.

And this is when Rejection Sensitive Dysphoria will be at its absolute finest. Their feelings of rejection will be crippling. It's difficult to explain just how painful it is but, trust me, it's a serious amount of pain your teenager will be going through. So they need extra delicate handling.

Now the next scenario, where the attraction is mutual, and your teenager is officially 'seeing' somebody. This might be a difficult conversation to have, but it's one that you need to. Remembering ADHD teens do things impulsively, without thinking of the consequences and enjoy risk-taking and thrill-seeking, you need to have the 'contraception conversation' with them as soon as you suspect they are seeing somebody.

The rate of teenage pregnancies is much higher with ADHD adolescents and I know plenty of ADHD adults who had their first child when they were 15 or 16.

So whether your teenager is male or female don't leave the contraception conversation too late. If you think it might be better had by an uncle, aunt or a family friend, then organise it with them.

But if you don't want your 15-year-old son getting his 14-year-old girlfriend pregnant you really need to be on the ball with this and have that conversation sooner rather than later.

If it's your daughter who is ADHD, I would strongly consider a trip with her to the GP or the sexual health clinic to have a good chat about what the options are. She might have absolutely no plans on sleeping with her boyfriend, but things can so easily go further when your brain is constantly looking for adrenaline, and it's much better she is protected and covered for all eventualities.

And then there's the awful scenario I have come across, where a teenage mutually consensual relationship suddenly turned into her having been raped when she reported it to the police several years later and the male ended up going to prison for it. So much as they might want to, and much as you might be open minded, it really is better to encourage your teenager to wait till the official age of consent.

Your ADHD teenager will be constantly looking for excitement, and that may mean they get bored with relationships very quickly and move onto the next boy or girl.

They also may hyper-focus on any new girlfriend or boyfriend and this can be very off-putting for some neurotypical partners. ADHD teenagers are likely to fall heavy and hard. Some potential partners will like it. Some will run a mile.

Emotional dysregulation also means most ADHD teenagers don't handle relationships well. They can get desperately upset if a text isn't returned quickly enough and can overthink any situation to the point of tears or even self-harm.

Not a nice statistic next, but one I wish I'd known in my late teens. ADHD women are much more susceptible to controlling and coercive relationships. I suspect ADHD men are, too, but as with domestic violence of any kind, it tends to be the women who are the victims. Classically, I fell into one of these aged 19. All the usual awful stuff went on – cutting me off from my friends and family, stopping me working, not letting me out of his sight etc, all of which

I let go. But when he punched me for the first time, I knew I had to get out. The second time he did it, shortly afterwards, I got out.

So please look out for this with your daughter and possibly your sons too. They'll hide it from you – I know I did. But our ADHD lack of self-esteem and people-pleasing tendencies mean we are ripe for the picking by these controlling types.

On a positive, if you have a teenage ADHD boy, a good strong, sensible girlfriend can massively keep them on the right path. I have seen this so many times. The right girlfriend can keep a strong-willed, risk-taking teenage ADHD boy on the straight and narrow more than any parent!

If this is sounding like a minefield, then it really is. You only have one job throughout all this. And that is to keep your teenager as regulated and safe as you possibly can. And also to be there with tissues and mugs of hot chocolate when your teen thinks the world has ended, which they will do on a regular basis.

Top Take-Aways

Crushes and first relationships are extremely difficult for ADHD teenagers. Their heightened emotions and ramped-up hormones during puberty mean they have a much more difficult time than other kids. Have some sympathy for them as they go through the ups and downs of first relationships because it really can be tumultuous and gut-wrenchingly painful.

Have the 'contraceptive talk' earlier than you would with neurotypical teenagers, who don't have the risk-taking and thrill-seeking ADHD traits constantly flooding through their brain.

Don't Bother ...

Thinking it's all something and nothing and will blow over. You could find yourself with a pregnant 12-year-old or a scared 13-year-old who has just found out his girlfriend is pregnant.

DAMAGE LIMITATION TARGETS:

35
GCSES – THE DREADED STUDYING, REVISION AND HOMEWORK

Round about the age of 14, in the UK at least, your teenager will be asked to consider what 'options' they would like to take for their GCSEs, the exams they take around the age of 16.

My best advice to you here is to be guided by your teen. Much as you might think a solid grounding in maths, English, a language and a science would be a good thing – if your teenager is dead set on doing theatre studies, history, art and drama, go with THEIR preference.

The reason for this is that their brain will only be stimulated and want to give any time and attention to subjects of interest to them. So if they have any hope of getting good marks, it is always going to be in the subjects that stimulate their brain. It's really not a good idea to force on them subjects that just don't interest them.

Their brain is not like a neurotypical brain. It won't be able to give equal interest to subjects across the board. It literally will only be interested in learning subjects that ignite some sort of passion in their ADHD brain cells.

Before they get to this point, it is crucial that they have had any ADHD coexisting conditions diagnosed, whether that is dyslexia, dyscalculia, dysgraphia or any other learning difficulty. It's critical because they will get the relevant support and allowances made for each condition. It might be they need more time, a break halfway through or it may be they need to study, or take an exam, in a separate room. So if you've been wondering whether they have any of these conditions but have not yet done anything about it, please do get these diagnoses in place before they start sitting exams.

Homework can be another big issue with some ADHD teenagers. I've met many who consider it an absolute outrage that they should be expected to do work at home when home is 'their home' and school is the place for school work. I have met some very indignant teenagers who absolutely refuse point blank to do homework at home.

Something you might want to keep to yourself is that homework is actually not obligatory in the UK. If your teenager is absolutely dead set against doing anything at home that resembles homework, encourage them to do it either on the bus into school or the bus home, at lunchtime or during breaks. If you make it sound like a choice – that they have the choice whether to do their homework when they get home OR to get it all out of the way while they're at school – I can almost guarantee which option they will take!

You will find the odd ADHD teenager who is like me. I used to race through the door, throw my satchel on the floor by my desk and crack straight on with my homework. I couldn't enjoy my evening until I knew that my homework had been done and was out of the way. These kids are relatively easy to deal with as they realise that homework is priority and will get it done first.

The procrastinators are more of a problem. They will put off homework until they have changed out of their school clothes, until they've had a drink, until they've had something to eat, until they've had half an hour on the iPad, then it becomes dinner time and then they don't want to do their homework until they've watched their favourite TV show and before you know it, it's bedtime and no homework has been done.

For these ADHD teens – and there are a lot of them – I strongly suggest you get a post-school routine going with ideally a very small reward at the end of it. So, for example, if they have done all their homework by 6 p.m., they can have some nuts and nibbles or Doritos and dips before dinner. Or they get to choose the pudding, or something that doesn't cost you any money but is a reward for them getting their homework done and out of the way so you don't have to spend the rest of your evening begging them to do it.

Another way to ensure homework gets done is to maybe organise one or two evenings a week where they work with a friend. Once a week at your house and once a week at theirs. And also, if you can afford it, a tutor, even once a week, will work wonders. Because the tutor will work at the same pace as your child and be 100% focused on only them. I've known teenagers to be struggling massively in some subjects and then within literally a few weeks of working with a tutor, the situation has been completely turned around and teachers and parents are staggered at the improvement.

Revision is something that is going to be particularly difficult for your ADHD teenager, especially if they aren't on medication. There is a very legitimate reason for this: an ADHD brain does not think a thought long enough for it to be stored as a memory. So just looking at text – that they have already looked at once before, so is therefore instantly boring and not stimulating to the brain – is very unlikely to work. What works better for revision is coming up with different ways of getting the information into their brain in a more innovative and stimulating way.

If we take English as an example: if they are studying a play, take them to see the live show in a theatre. If there is a DVD version, invest in that. Or an audiobook version, buy that. If the play is set in Cornwall, take them to Cornwall for a couple of weeks on holiday. Get them to listen to the book or read it while they are actually in the play's location. And anything online is always going to stimulate your child. So if there is a YouTube version or an actor talking about the play or some students performing it, then they are likely to absorb that much more successfully than they are reading a book.

If your teenager is determined to revise from text, then encourage them to do it in small chunks with a reward after every 30 minutes, or maybe 45 minutes. It can just be a milkshake and a biscuit or a cup of tea and a slice of cake. But they will work much better in small chunks with a small reward after each one. Also expect them to revise and take in information last minute. No self-respecting ADHD person can revise six months in advance. Plenty CAN revise six days in advance so that information is much more likely to stay in.

When it comes to actually taking GCSEs, it's very standard for a lot of ADHD kids to think they're going to do abysmally, because they just haven't managed to revise as much as their peers and their low self-esteem makes them think they are going to balls the whole lot up. However, I have good news.

At GCSE level, often ADHD kids do way better than expected. This is because GCSEs are by and large a lot of common sense and if you can waffle well about a subject – and most ADHD kids can chat for England – they will usually breeze through their GCSEs and get much higher results than they are expecting. GCSEs aren't usually the problem. It's the next level that becomes a problem!

Top Take-Aways

Allow your child to study subjects that stimulate their brain. Be creative with revision techniques. Consider a tutor.

Don't Bother ...

Putting six-month revision plans in place or expecting your child to sit down with a textbook and absorb information. They will revise much better at the last minute, and by using more stimulating methods to get the information into their brain.

DAMAGE LIMITATION TARGETS:

36
A LEVELS. NOW THINGS GET A BIT TOUGHER – AND WHY DROPPING HISTORY IS USUALLY A WINNER

When you have counselled as many ADHD teenagers as I have, you definitely do see patterns. Kids who have sailed through their GCSEs suddenly come to a grinding half about three months into their A levels. And it's always for the same reasons. I've analysed this with dozens of teenagers over the years and we've come to the same conclusion. For starters there are fewer subjects. So it's just not as exciting or varied is it?

Before, they were going into school studying ten or more different subjects a week. Now suddenly, it's reduced to three or four, maximum. So already that has become boring.

Also the time for waffling and general knowledge is gone. Now it gets a lot more serious – not helped in my opinion by some teachers putting the fear of God into teens, telling them that the time for easy exams has long gone; A levels are a different thing entirely. Forget all thoughts of enjoying lessons, having a laugh with the teacher and sailing through exams; now it's all deadly serious, very intense study and their entire life and future depends on them passing these A levels.

This sort of pressure and intensity has brought numerous broken, weeping teenagers into my therapy room, convinced they are doomed from the start, with parents petrified they are about to throw their future down the toilet, but also terrified for their teenager's delicate mental health.

The way I have played it in therapy is the way I would recommend with your teenager. First of all don't make them feel they have made their bed and have to lie in it. Their life does not depend on them passing these A levels. If they have made the wrong choice and should have instead gone down the vocational route, and now decide they actually want to be a plumber or a hairdresser, it is not too late.

Don't let them feel trapped and that there is no way out of this situation. Because from feeling trapped can come dangerous feelings of looking for ways out and we don't want your teenager ever to feel that there is just no way out of a situation. There is always a way out.

If you are dealing with this situation without a therapist, I strongly recommend you take the pressure off. Keep them off school for a week, or however long it takes to have a jolly good think about what they actually want in life. Ideally whisk them off to the seaside or even for a week abroad. Take them right away from the situation so they can really think about it when they are distanced from it.

If they still do want to take all these chosen A levels then that's absolutely fine and you need to find a way that is going to work for them. Going back in with a 'new attitude' can sometimes be all it takes. Knowing that their life and future does not depend on passing these A levels can be enough for them to decide it's worth going back, giving it their best and accepting that's good enough.

I always stress if they decide to go back they are literally 'having a go'. Nothing is set in stone. If they go back and a week later decide they've made a mistake they must feel able to tell you.

And what has happened in nearly every scenario I've worked with is that the teenagers have decided to drop one of their subjects. I've had teenagers go from taking four A levels to three and from three A levels to two. And this is when dropping history has become a much recurring theme! Much as I adored history, so please don't think I'm slating it, when it comes to A levels, it seems that history is the one that every ADHD teenager wants to drop. I honestly cannot remember any ADHD clients dropping any other subject.

Also, please don't think that by dropping A levels, even down to two, this limits their prospects. The honest truth is that one of my clients who had this sort of 'It's too much I can't cope' crisis, after much angst, dropped down from three to two A levels and is now in his final years of training to be a doctor. And yes, he dropped history!

While your teen is going through this it is very important to keep the lines of communication open, always checking that they aren't finding things too much. Remind them that they can change their mind at any point and nobody will think any less of them, that their happiness and mental wellbeing is the only thing that matters and not to get too bogged down in the pressures school might be putting on them.

Most entrepreneurs haven't been to university or taken A levels. This is a good time to remind them of that fact. A lot of entrepreneurs left school at 15 or 16, without a qualification to their name, and went on to become multi-millionaires and world leaders in the fields of technology, business, television, sport, theatre and a hundred other professions. And a very large chunk of that number, if not all of them, are ADHD.

So carrying on with A levels IS one option, but there ARE always others. This is the message you need to keep getting through to them right the way through. There is always a way out if they need it.

Once the pressure is off and they know there won't be any repercussions if they change their mind (and usually when they have dropped history!) you'll be staggered how many ADHD teenagers get back on track and pass with flying colours.

Overwhelm has always featured in these 'wobbly A levels' teenagers. Keeping up with oceans of homework, other kids who can revise when they struggle and the lack of stimulation needed for their brain to function when they've dropped from twelve subjects to three, means overwhelm is nearly always the root cause of the anxiety.

Top Take-Aways

A levels are a very different ballgame to GCSEs. Expect the pressure to ramp up on your teenager and be prepared to deal with the repercussions.

Keep the lines of communication open, don't be judgmental about what they can or can't cope with and always let them know that their happiness and wellbeing is paramount. They can achieve in life with or without A levels (especially history!).

Don't Bother …

Putting extra pressure on them. Reminding them how their older brother or sister sailed through their A levels. Making them feel bad if they need to drop a subject.

DAMAGE LIMITATION TARGETS:

37
UNIVERSITY – HOLD ONTO YOUR MORTARBOARDS

If they've smashed their A levels and made it to university, you might think you are home and dry. But actually now is the time to be on your guard more than ever before. Because if your teenager has held it all together up till now, it could be in the next three years that all the wheels fall off – or at least some of them! And there are a lot of very good ADHD-related reasons for this.

Of course, there are plenty who go to university, have an absolute ball, are academically brilliant and come out with a first or any degree they are extremely proud of. There are thousands of these ADHD graduates out there, so please don't assume everything is going to go horribly wrong. I only like to warn people of the worst-case scenarios in case they crop up. And all I'm about to tell you has cropped up with some of my ADHD clients.

Before they even go to university, in Year 13 at school, that's the time to start putting support in place for them. Firstly, apply for DSA – Disabled Students' Allowance. There is a huge amount of support available and this is the best place to start – this will almost always include a mentor or even a counsellor.

Also start talking to the University Disability Support teams before they get there, to help with the transition. The Student Union may well have a Disability Advisor or even possibly a Neurodiversity

Inclusion Officer – well worth seeking them out beforehand, as they'll be a mine of information and will have insider info on that particular university and who it's best to speak to for help.

Each teenager will have very different challenges and support will need to be highly personal but the sort of things on offer will be:

- Laptops
- Printers
- Dragon Dictation Software
- Customised chairs and desks

Some teens are terrified of meeting these kinds of 'authority' figures, but do assure them the advisors are on their side. It their job to make your teen's life at uni more accessible. The only evidence you will need to access this support in their diagnosis letter(s) or report(s).

At home, in the months before they leave for uni, make sure their 'life skills' are up to scratch. Particularly if your teen has never been near the kitchen or opened the washing machine. Doing their own laundry, cooking, shopping, budgeting and banking is best learnt in that last year, or gap year, before they take the giant leap into looking after themselves.

If your son or daughter is going to a local university and decides to stay at home to save costs, and you are wondering if that is a good idea, the answer is yes. Keeping a bit of structure in their life is an exceptionally good idea. It's when kids go off and live in halls or shared houses away from all structure and routine that things can get rocky.

If they do go away, sometimes very far away, keep an eye out for homesickness especially in the first couple of terms. Never underestimate how crippling homesickness can be. I had it when I went travelling to Australia for a year and it made me beyond miserable for several weeks. Really miserable. 'Calling the Samaritans' miserable.

Having contact to look forward to really helps, so factor in more telephone calls, face-times, visits to them and them coming home where possible. Emotional dysregulation can hit hard when first away but if you support them through it, with plenty of contact, hopefully they'll settle. Also – knowing they don't HAVE to stay is a good tactic. If you let them know this, that they always have CHOICES, they know there's a way out and that alone makes it easier to stay.

The first problem is usually that all boundaries and structure have been removed. So there is no teacher telling them what class to be in and when. There is no parent telling them to do their homework, what to eat and when to go to bed. Much as ADHD people kick against rules and structure we actually function much better in them. So this newfound freedom means ADHD teens are likely to make the most of all the opportunities open to them.

And oh, what a lot of opportunities there are! Alcohol on tap. Probably drugs on tap just as easily. Promiscuity – all suddenly becoming available and the norm. You may find their risk-taking and thrill-seeking suddenly rockets to new levels.

A lot of ADHD adolescents don't have their first full sexual relationships until they get to university and once they start feeling the adrenaline rush, the thrill of the chase, the excitement and buzz of a new relationship, it's very difficult to stop. So your swotty teenager, who may not have shown much interest in romantic relationships, may suddenly become a Casanova overnight.

If your teenager hasn't been on medication, or has come off it, and starts to show a lot of this sort of behaviour, it's a very good idea to bring up the subject of medication again. It will most definitely curb if not eradicate their desire for alcohol and illegal substances and will also make them think of the consequences of any risk-taking, boundary-pushing or thrill-seeking activities they are getting up to.

I've heard some classic stories of ADHD people at university. One of our very own Headstuff coaches was awarded a cup for 'The Student Attending Least Lectures' over his three-year English literature degree. And this was at the third university he had even tried to get his degree at! Which he finally managed to, barely attending a lecture.

Also to be expected is your teen deciding they are on the wrong course. This very same coach of ours changed his mind TWICE and came out with a degree on a very different subject to the one he started with! I've met numerous ADHD teens who started studying drama and switched to classics after three months or equally dramatic swaps!

So if your teen calls you up wailing, 'I've made a terrible mistake,' do take them seriously. Staying on the wrong course will just make them despondent and if the subject matter is not stimulating their brain, you're flogging a dead horse forcing them to stay on something they've gone off.

Another ADHD girl I know started university doing English and history. After two years she was thrown off the history course and had to restart again doing purely English. She managed another two years English and then was thrown off that course as well – for not attending lectures and not handing in any work. So she spent four years at university and came away with absolutely nothing. That is not unusual. She just didn't have the motivation to finish because she wasn't medicated.

Lack of organisation often becomes a problem when teenagers go to university. Usually for the first time they have to organise their own life – their own laundry, their own shopping, their own cooking, their own cleaning – on top of all the university work. For some this is just too much and they get cripplingly overwhelmed.

Many get into debt because they haven't learnt how to manage money and a lot of them throw the towel in because it's all just too much to manage. Somebody I know who found himself in that situation became a lorry driver instead, and was very happy for the rest of his life, driving around the country delivering pork pies with no pressure.

Your teen may now think the time has come for partying hard and 'who needs sleep anyway'. Well *they* do! And if they don't get it, a lot will become tired and emotional – much more emotional. And with their emotional dysregulation, this can be seriously not a good idea.

So listen out for signs of haywire sleeping patterns if your teen is suddenly a lot more emotional. Checking up on how much sleep they're getting is a very good idea. Subtly, of course. Never telling them what to do, but maybe with some helpful suggestions!

If you feel your son or daughter is struggling, and if you can afford it, now is a very good time to book them in with an ADHD coach, one who specialises in working with students who are studying. We have those on our team. This can be a huge weight off your teenager's shoulders: to have somebody who is on their side, collaboratively coming up with new ways of organising their life. Then they don't feel so helpless and useless. A good coach can help structure everything for them, so that they have time for pleasure and leisure, but have their life in order and still achieve academically.

It can be done, but a lot of ADHD teenagers just don't have the ability to do it for themselves so an ADHD student specialist coach is a brilliant idea.

Top Take-Aways

Be prepared for your teenager to find things unexpectedly very difficult and different. Support them as much as you can without taking over. Make suggestions as to how they can plan and organise their life, or book them in with an ADHD coach who can do the same for them.

Don't Bother …

Thinking they will manage, adapt easily to a completely new way of living and there won't be any hiccups along the way. That's highly unlikely.

Your role is to be there in the background, fully supportive, non-judgmental, and to encourage them to either get back on or start ADHD medication and potentially seek help from an ADHD coach.

DAMAGE LIMITATION TARGETS:

38
CAREERS AND JOB CHOICES

Deciding what they want to do can be a very big problem for some ADHD adolescents. In fact, I know a lot of ADHD adults who say that making a decision is the hardest thing they ever have to do, so if your teenager hasn't a clue what they want to do with their life, don't be particularly concerned about it. In those circumstances, I encourage them to take whatever qualifications are going to keep their options open as much as possible. Because one thing we are very good at is changing our mind, so limiting your options, qualifications wise, is not a good idea.

There are a few tips that might help you guide your teenager in the right direction. ADHD people don't like doing the same thing over and over again. They like jobs with variety, where they can move about, when no two days are the same, and in an ideal world where there is some adrenaline involved. So you will actually find a lot of ADHD people working in the fire service, the police forces and also particularly as ambulance drivers and paramedics.

Paramedic is allegedly the best job for an ADHD person. Because it combines two very important things. Firstly excitement, adrenaline and drama when you are called to a new emergency, never knowing what you are going to find when you get there. And ADHD brains work best in a crisis. A neurotypical brain flooded with adrenaline will often freeze. But an ADHD brain flooded with adrenaline will see things more clearly and be able to act more quickly than neurotypicals.

And secondly our extra dollop of compassion makes us extremely good at dealing with people who are hurt or in distress. So if your teen shows any leanings towards training to be a nurse, doctor, paramedic or anything in the caring professions, they have almost definitely made a sensible choice. You will find lots of ADHD adults working as social workers, counsellors, mental health nurses and carers.

If your child shows any culinary skills, encourage that because allegedly the second-top job for ADHD people is chef. I don't think we need to look much further than Gordon Ramsay and Heston Blumenthal to know why. Again, no two days are the same, creativity is welcomed, looking after and pleasing the public is involved, and it's a high-adrenaline environment.

I've met many ADHD young men who have trained as plumbers, electricians, carpenters, bricklayers, landscape gardeners, roofers and scaffolders, who make a very good living from physical work. Again, these people like being out and about, on the road, not tied to one place with no two days being the same. So if your teenager has a yearning to be an electrician or plumber, it's definitely worth encouraging.

For ADHD girls, and of course also some boys, who like looking after themselves, a lot of them find themselves training to be beauticians, hairdressers or nail technicians. Again, these professions will have them working with the public, caring for them, making them look better, chatting to them – and no two days are the same so these are good career options. Even better, once they are trained, they can take their skills off around the world, working on cruise ships, in international hotels, for holiday companies and can also very easily be self-employed which brings us nicely onto the next category.

A huge proportion of ADHD people are self-employed. This is because we don't like being told what to do. We don't like authority, we think we know best and we want everything our own way. So self-employment is the way to go. I remember going in to employment agencies from a very young age and looking at the lady across the desk thinking 'I want to be where you are. I want to be sitting there helping people find jobs'. So at 17 the lady on the other side of the desk told me to go and get more experience and come back in a couple of years.

By the time I was 23, I found myself working in an employment agency and I absolutely loved it, because it combined my two loves: coming first and winning – which I did every time I made a successful placement – and also helping people. I loved nothing more than rushing to the aid of people who arrived in floods of tears because they had been made redundant or had been fired from their job and then I would place them in a job that was better paid and would completely transform their life. That gave me huge amounts of satisfaction.

My finest moment was when a 30-year-old girl rang up crying on a Monday afternoon because she had just been made redundant and she was due to move into her first owned property on the Friday. She was absolutely devastated and terrified: how she would pay the mortgage? By the Wednesday, I had placed her in a better-paid job that she started the following Monday. That was what gave me my buzz and my adrenaline, and kept me away from drugs and alcohol I suspect. It also saw me thinking I knew better than my previous two bosses and starting up my own agency when I was 25. Believe it or not it still exists to this day, thirty-five years later, only it now specialises in recruiting staff for neurodiverse clients.

You will find a lot of ADHD adults working in recruitment and sales environments, which are very people focused and where there is an adrenaline rush when they make a sale. ADHD people are often extremely good at sales. I've known 19-year-old ADHD boys be making thousands of pounds a month because they are so good at selling.

ADHD people feel a strong need to be in charge of their day. They don't like to be micromanaged. They don't like to have their diaries dictated by someone else. They like to be autonomous. This can be very difficult when you're young and in your first job, but it gets easier the more experienced and older you get.

It's absolutely not a coincidence when they say all entrepreneurs are ADHD. Richard Branson, Jamie Oliver, will.i.am and just about every other entrepreneur you can think of is either diagnosed or rumoured to be ADHD.

Also, think sport. If you have a teen who is excelling or particularly passionate about one particular sport, then encourage them to follow their dream. I've worked with teenage girl professional golfers, boys on rugby scholarships, young boys training to be footballers and all sorts of other sporting activities. If their one and only passion is hockey or netball or basketball then let them follow it. Even if they don't end up playing professionally they may play in a junior team or they might become a coach or a physiotherapist or something else in that industry. So allow your teenager to focus on what they are passionate about. And that might not necessarily be just one thing. A lot of ADHD people have at least two businesses on the go.

And something else to remember, ADHD people are not good in positions where their earnings are capped. They like to know the sky is the limit and the harder they push themselves, the more determined they are to win, the more money or benefits there are at the end of it, the better.

It can be quite demoralising for an ADHD brain, knowing however good you are and how much you excel in a month you are always going to get the same amount of money at the end of it. In fact, I know a whole branch of an employment agency who walked out when the management put that policy in. The high earners were so disgusted that they would be supporting the lower earners. I suspect a few if not all of them were ADHD!

Top Take-Aways

Don't force your teenager into a career if they really can't make their mind up. Keep their options open and allow them to try lots of different jobs before they settle on one, or even two or three, that they want to focus on.

Remind them that, however pretty a boutique is, are they going to want to sit in it for forty hours a week? Probably not. More likely something where they are out and about and moving around is going to keep them better stimulated.

Don't Bother …

Getting aeriated and irritated if your teenager chops and changes jobs more often than you think is good for their CV. They will get bored very quickly and they will know when something really isn't right for them and will then be itching to move onto something new.

Accept that while they're in their teens and their 20s this is very probably what their career is going to look like until they find 'their thing'. And that may well be more than one thing. And it may well mean being self-employed.

DAMAGE LIMITATION TARGETS:

39
MANAGING MONEY – OR MORE LIKELY, NOT!

Money, managing bills and budgeting can be a major problem and an absolute nightmare for a lot of ADHD people, and especially for teenagers who have been used to having parents control their finances.

I know what happened when I went to work in London at 17, and started earning very good money – even by London standards! It was the first time I had had big money in my life, and I got myself into debt. I couldn't cope with being paid every four weeks and having a whopping great amount arrive in my bank. It was mostly gone within a fortnight. The excitement and newness of having all that money meant it was spent within days.

So let's first look at the traits that impact ADHD people and their finances.

The first one has to be impulsivity. We are shocking for not being able to say no when something looks exciting and enticing. I could write a whole book on my impulsive purchases over the years. And truthfully, most of it was rubbish. There are houses and cars in there, which mostly weren't, but there's an awful lot of tat that just appealed to my impulsive brain.

The adrenaline buzz we get from buying something is incredibly powerful and shouldn't be underestimated. I remember even as a little girl going to the shops with my mum, which felt like a complete and utter waste of time UNLESS I was promised a treat or some sweets from the supermarket – the excitement literally lit up my head which started buzzing with anticipation.

Next we have the ADHD trait of wanting everything now. ADHD people just do not want to wait, so they would rather get into debt, borrow money or run up huge credit card bills to have what they want right now, with no waiting. We can inattentively not notice those nasty credit card bills mounting up because they're not interesting!

Those of us with the ADHD coexisting condition of dyscalculia have the added issue of not really liking or understanding numbers. The severity of this condition and the areas of mathematics and finances affected are different for each of us. But I know I have always found bank and credit card statements interminably boring and very difficult to interpret – and as for company accounts, don't get me started. I won't even go near them. So teenagers with dyscalculia may well be very uninterested in what their bank statement or credit card statement tells them, and much more interested in what their next purchase is!

Believe it or not compassion, and our extra dollop, comes into this category as well. We will give money away to people, lend money to people who are crying because they can't pay a bill, donate to homeless people on the streets as I used to in my early 20s, when I didn't have much money of my own, and we will give away our last coin if it helps somebody who desperately needs it.

Hoarding can become a problem for some teenagers and, having lived with one, I strongly recommend you stamp it out as soon as possible, because it's going to make them very unpopular with partners! This is when impulsivity goes seriously haywire. Some ADHD people literally cannot stop picking up ANYTHING whether they pay for it, steal it or take things for free from the skip at the back of a shop; they will literally pick up anything and everything that catches their eye. They won't have the willpower not to. But if their room starts getting overwhelmed by 'stuff' it's time to have a good chat with them about only buying what they absolutely need and perhaps donating the rest to charity, which appeals to their compassionate side.

Money usually becomes a big problem for ADHD teens either when they go to university or when they leave home. It just doesn't seem to stretch far enough! The very best way I have found of helping teenagers help themselves with this is to start them working from a young age. This can be very young. Literally 9- and 10-year-olds can earn a little bit of money by helping you in the garden, or by washing the car, or by emptying the dishwasher every night. If they start to earn money very young, and you encourage them to spend some and save some, it will get them in the right mindset as they grow up.

Teenagers should be encouraged to work, I firmly believe. Again, if you prefer this to be round the home that's fine, but I think it does them better to get an actual job from around the age of 13. Obviously part-time and definitely one that doesn't impact their studies, but it will get them in the habit of earning money, and more importantly controlling their own money. If you see that they are earning a good wage from working at the local burger bar on Saturdays and Sundays and have spent it by Tuesday – you will soon know that having a conversation about how to manage money is going to benefit them.

And one thing I have to warn you about. There is no bigger money to be made than by selling drugs. It's quite mind-boggling the money teenagers can make from selling or 'carrying' drugs and I have known numerous teenagers who have done this, despite my best efforts to stop them. I am always absolutely terrified they will be arrested and sent to prison. Some of them I have met in young offender units. But the lure of money from selling drugs can be VERY powerful, so if your child starts going out at strange times and coming back hiding packages please do jump on it as quickly as you can. I've seen numerous 13- and 14-year-olds become involved in drug dealing because the financial rewards are breathtakingly high.

There are some ADHD teens who are absolutely fantastic at managing their money, but this is a much smaller category. You will find some start a part-time job and save like crazy, bank all their birthday and Christmas money and get huge satisfaction from seeing their savings grow. But for the rest, you will need to encourage them to understand which of their ADHD traits are going to impact on them financially and instil a good work ethic into them from as young an age as you possibly can.

Top Take-Aways

Money is nearly always a problem for ADHD teenagers. Earning their own and learning to manage it from a young age is always a good idea. Help them decide how much they need and how much they want to save and encourage them to open up savings accounts as a youngster.

Don't Bother ...

Making them save absolutely everything they earn. They will soon see this as pointless. Let them be frivolous with a portion, buying whatever they want, as long as they are saving some.

DAMAGE LIMITATION TARGETS:

40
MEDICATION – AND WHY IT CAN BE CRITICAL

It's not uncommon for teenagers to have come off their ADHD medication – if they were ever on it. This is usually for one of the following reasons:

- Because they have been told that 'they will have outgrown their ADHD now they are in their late teens and don't need to take medication anymore'. This is one of the urban myths that is most dangerous.

- Because they see taking ADHD medication as a childhood/kiddy type of thing, and it's not very cool or grown up when you are 19.

- Because they have been on it for so long they have started to think that how they feel is normal and don't realise that actually their new normal is because of the ADHD medication.

- Because their parents have struggled to get them transferred from children's services to adult services at 18. Sometimes it's easier to just stop taking the medication than to fight a broken healthcare system (as I write in 2023. We can only hope that ADHD services improve because they really can't be much worse).

- Because of the cost. If parents have been paying privately, they may now think that their teen is out of education and reasonably grown up, they might not need the medication for concentrating and focusing so much.

In my experience, this is nearly always a big mistake; it can actually be a life-changing mistake and never in a good way.

I cannot begin to tell you the number of teenagers I have worked with who have come off their ADHD medication and soon after plonked themselves back in my therapy room, telling me how their life has gone hideously wrong. Not one of them has linked this to the fact that they have come off their ADHD medication, but they do know their life is now in chaos. They are either bingeing on alcohol or drugs, selling them sometimes, have been taking massive risks or have been arrested! A couple have even had heart attacks as teenagers because of the amount of drugs they've been taking.

So let's debunk a few myths. ADHD is not a childhood behavioural disorder and you most certainly do not outgrow it in your late teens. You are as ADHD the day you die as the day you are born. This is in the vast majority of cases, not taking acquired brain injury into account but that really is a very small minority.

So while it might be a battle to keep your ADHD teenager on medication, I strongly recommend you do. It is going to protect them in so many ways.

Crucially, it is going to stop their impulsivity and allow them to think of the consequences of their actions.

They won't be so inattentive so won't be walking into a busy road or falling off cliffs. Their distraction won't be so strong and the hyperactivity and boredom levels will be manageable rather than forcing them outside to get involved in who knows what.

Their risk-taking and thrill-seeking will be managed as they will have enough adrenaline in their brain not to be constantly seeking the buzz.

On top of this if they are driving or riding motorbikes they are going to be much safer on ADHD medication because distraction and inattention can cause an awful lot of road traffic accidents.

They are also going to be protected from excessive drinking and drug taking because their adrenaline-seeking brain will be satisfied by the medication and not crave illicit substances.

If your teenager has started to be sexually active, they will be less likely to have promiscuous sex, be less at risk of either getting pregnant or getting somebody pregnant unintentionally, sexually transmitted infections will be less likely, and very importantly, they will be protected from most offending behaviour.

For those who struggle with binge eating, like me pre-meds, and find their adrenaline in food, it will also protect them from putting on stones in weight. And I mean stones. I have known ADHD people reach between 30 and 40 stone in weight due to uncontrolled binge eating.

For teenagers who have started to work, they will find focusing and concentrating at work much easier and will also be able to take instructions from superiors without wanting to snap back at them or walk out of their job if they disagree with a decision.

And when it comes to anger – being on the ADHD medication will allow them to manage their inner rage and frustrations so much better. I have met many teenagers in prison who have punched somebody ONCE and been unlucky enough for the person to be either seriously injured or even killed. So your teenager not on medication, by having a few pints and a bit of a punch up outside the pub after work on a Friday – could find themselves banged up for eight years. I've met these people. They do exist. They were all ADHD and my heart broke for how easily and stupidly they'd ended up in prison.

So to avoid all this, it really is worth pushing to keep your teenager on their ADHD medication until they are well out of their teenage years.

This is before we even touch on emotional dysregulation, and how that can lead to self-harm and even suicide. I don't like to put the fear of God into people over this because it is rare and I was very lucky enough until this most recent year not to have lost a client to suicide. But that changed in 2023, when one of my most precious young offenders became so emotionally dysregulated he took his own life. He was not on ADHD medication despite my best efforts to get him back on it.

So for these and numerous other reasons, I strongly recommend you work hard to keep your ADHD teenager medicated. I've known parents have the most colossal battles to get ADHD teenagers to agree to take their medication, but it really is worth the fight because I've seen the dreadful results of unmedicated ADHD.

I quite appreciate there are side-effects, but there are now more and more choices of ADHD medication that might work differently so please don't ever give up trying to get your ADHD teenager to take medication.

Top Take-Aways

Medication is nearly always a very good idea for ADHD teenagers and young adults. There is an extensive list of ways in which it can help them and, most importantly, protect them.

Don't Bother …

Listening to people who say that ADHD is a childhood behavioural disorder. They are clueless about the condition and how it affects you all your life. Nor people who say taking ADHD medication leads to addiction. All the research points to the polar opposite – it protects you FROM addiction.

DAMAGE LIMITATION TARGETS:

41
SLEEP PROBLEMS, INSOMNIA AND DELAYED SLEEP PHASE SYNDROME

Sleep can be an absolutely massive problem for a lot of ADHD people, me included, and I'm going to give you my very best advice on how to help your teenager if they are struggling to nod off or waking up numerous times during the night or waking up far too early.

First of all, let's look at this condition called 'Delayed Sleep Phase Syndrome'. For those of us old enough to remember the Duracell bunny adverts on the television, an ADHD brain has the equivalent of a Duracell battery in it, meaning our brains go on for longer than average. This can mean that your teenager will be wide awake and functioning fantastically at one or two in the morning which can be very frustrating if you are a household who likes to close down for the night at 10 p.m.

DSPS has affected me all my life. Everybody who knows me knows I despise mornings, I never arrange meetings in them and I don't even like being awake in the morning as it makes the day drag terribly! To this day I don't go to sleep till at least 1 a.m. and like to emerge somewhere around 11 a.m.!

So you thinking your teenager is a lazy layabout who won't get up in the mornings because they won't go to bed early enough at night, could actually be connected to this genuine sleep condition.

DSPS is caused when somebody's circadian rhythm is off-kilter. So while another person may get sleepy at 10 p.m. or 11 p.m., the ADHD brain with its Duracell bunny battery can happily go on till at least 1 or 2 a.m. and for some people 3 or 4 a.m. I am my best at 1 a.m., which is why so many people get emails from me at that time. At 9 a.m. – not a hope!

You might also think your teen needs to sort this out before they enter the world of college or work because surely they won't be able to function in 'normal society'? However, I have made it work my entire life because I didn't have a choice. When I was working in offices I always offered to work the late shift as plenty wanted to start at 8 a.m. and finish by 4 p.m. I managed to drag myself into the office by 10 a.m., which was still hideously early for me, but never minded working till six or seven in the evening.

I then worked as the Manager's PA in a nightclub where we didn't have to start until after 4 p.m., and since being self-employed from the age of 25 I've just told clients that 'I'm busy in the mornings on the phone and to catch me in the afternoons and evenings'. I've just given away my secret there. I always tell people that the phones are manic and I'm working in the mornings, but actually I'm asleep.

Then we have the polar opposite ADHD people. Very often those diagnosed with Inattentive ADHD like my brother, are permanently tired and cannot get enough sleep. Eleven years younger than me, he used to amaze us when he first started work in his late teens. He would come home from work on a Friday, go straight to bed, sleep solidly all weekend and then get up on Monday and go to work! And – more incredulously – still be tired! Some teenagers are permanently tired, no matter how much sleep they get.

Your teen may fall asleep in lessons in school especially if the room is very warm, the subject is boring them or the teacher isn't engaging enough. Well worth mentioning why this might occur with your teen to their school if they start getting told off for falling asleep in classes.

There are lots of things that help with sleep and I will give you my very best ideas here.

Firstly, don't be surprised if your teenager uses cannabis to help them sleep. I am not recommending it and I have never used it myself, but I have sat in front of trillions of teenagers who tell me that it is only by smoking cannabis in the evenings that they can calm their brain down enough to sleep. So have some sympathy with your adolescent if they are using cannabis purely to sleep.

However, there is little doubt it is not good for your brain cells and it can be the gateway to stronger and harder drugs so it's not something I would ever recommend long term. Not even medium term. Maybe short term just while you put some other things in place.

There are some brilliant, cheap and legal ways that really do help with sleep, so encourage your teenager to consider any or all of these.

First up would be melatonin. This can absolutely transform some children's and adolescent's sleep problems. Ask your doctor and you shouldn't have too much problem getting it if your child is either diagnosed ADHD or on a waiting list for an assessment. I believe you can also buy melatonin gummies from places like Amazon, and I've heard many parents say that this has revolutionised their child's sleep pattern.

Next I'm going to strongly recommend sleep hypnosis. I use this every night and have done for the best part of 20 years. Played 'on loop' which means it goes on constantly all night, your teen has the choice of dozens of free sleep hypnosis apps, and they can pick the one that makes them sleepiest. I strongly recommend you play this as close to their head as possible, but definitely not under the pillow because devices have been known to explode and we certainly don't want that. But close by on the bedside table or, if they don't have one, on the floor next to the bed is a very good idea.

Next we have aromatherapy. I burn sleep-inducing oils next to my bed every single night. I recommend a plug-in one because you don't really want a lit candle anywhere near an accident-prone ADHD teenager. The electric diffusers are much safer. You can buy all sorts of sleep-inducing oils in ready-prepared bottles, or if you want to be very entrepreneurial and become an apothecary, you can concoct your own. The sort of oils that work are chamomile, lavender, sandalwood and vetiver – there are a whole host of others. You can buy these bottles of oil pretty much everywhere online, including eBay and Amazon. They're becoming so mainstream that many supermarkets now sell ready-mixed sleep oils and the electric diffusers to use them in.

On a similar vein is sleep pillow spray. I also use this, sprayed liberally on the pillow before I sleep. It gives you a very nice relaxing smell wafting up your nostrils at close range. There are also roller balls that you can slather on your wrists or temples all with the same aim of these lovely sleepy smells relaxing you.

Another idea that works for a lot of people is a weighted blanket. I've no idea of the science behind this, but I do know that I cannot sleep with just a light duvet or sheet on top of me. Even in the hottest of weather I have to have a blanket for the weight. This is no doubt something to do with the common ADHD coexisting condition of sensory processing disorder, but I know a lot of us cannot sleep unless we have something like a weighted blanket on top of us. Please beware of cowboys who charge a fortune for these; you can get your local seamstress to run you up one much cheaper – you just need to do your research online as to what weight it needs to be.

Something that works very well for a lot of people, me included, is to have a fan on all night. There is something about the white noise that helps our brain relax and also for people who are always hot, even in the winter, the cooling of the fan is welcome too.

Another issue that can affect a lot of ADHD people is something called 'anticipation anxiety'. This is when we find it very difficult to sleep if we know we have something important to do the next day. 'Important' can be an exam, doing a public speech, starting at a new school, college or job or anything slightly out of what is normal for us. Anticipation anxiety can keep your teenager up all night and is yet another issue that affects me. Anti-anxiety medication might be the answer to this if it's an ongoing problem for your teenager, and doctors will often prescribe something like mirtazapine that can help your adolescent overcome the anxiety of getting to sleep at night.

Lack of sleep can be dangerous and I have known many ADHD teenagers and adults go 4–5 nights with no sleep at all. If this happens, make sure your adolescent sees the GP urgently. All their ADHD traits will be heightened if they aren't sleeping, so their inattention, distraction, not concentrating and not being able to focus will mean they are at risk.

Worst-case scenario – lack of sleep can also bring on psychosis. So please don't accept your teenager saying that 'everything will be fine' and they are 'quite happy playing on the PlayStation all night and getting no sleep'. If this goes on for more than two or three nights you need to frogmarch them into the GP and insist they are honest about what the issues are about getting to sleep and staying asleep.

Top Take-Aways

Sleep can be a huge problem so comments, like 'if you wanted to sleep, you would be able to' or 'it's just a question of closing your eyes and the sleep will come' really aren't helpful.

Don't Bother …

Ignoring it, letting them use cannabis long-term or hoping this is just a teenage thing that will get better. It's highly unlikely that's the case and you may need to try a lot of different methods of getting your teenager's brain to relax enough to sleep.

DAMAGE LIMITATION TARGETS:

42
EATING DISORDERS – AND WHY THEY ARE MORE LIKELY FOR ADHD TEENS

Now before I start this chapter, I'm going to make clear again what you probably have gathered and already know, but it's very important I stress this before we start talking about eating disorders.

I am in no way clinically or medically trained. I am not a GP, clinician or eating disorder specialist of any kind. What I am going to do here is explain to you how disordered eating can be connected to ADHD, but if you suspect your teenager has any sort of serious issues around eating, I strongly recommend you seek professional advice. This can come in many shapes and forms.

Your GP is a good place to start and an ADHD-specific therapist who specialises and is trained in eating disorders is also a good place to start. But do take it seriously because in worst-case scenarios this can be life-threatening.

There is a well-documented higher rate of eating disorders in teenagers with ADHD and there are some very good reasons for this. Let's start with the compulsive element of the brain. One of the ways an ADHD brain gets its adrenaline, dopamine or 'happiness injection' is through food. This can so easily lead onto compulsive or binge eating, something I battled with until I started ADHD medication in 2015.

This can be very perplexing for your teenager, and it's important they know that if for any reason they aren't on ADHD medication – and there can be lots of good reasons why they aren't – their brain is going to be compulsive and one of the ways it will get what it craves is from food. Because food is probably the most accessible, legal and easy way to give the brain adrenaline.

What can be very perplexing for your teenager is why they can't stop eating. I know this puzzled me for the best part of thirty years. Once my mother had stopped feeding me, and I was in charge of my own food intake, right up until my 50s when I first took ADHD medication, I struggled hugely with compulsive eating. It even used to perplex my friends. Puzzled, they'd say, 'You are so in control of everything else and achieving exactly what you want to achieve yet the one thing you can't control is your weight.'

They were absolutely right, but none of us were clever enough to know that this was because I had undiagnosed ADHD and a very compulsive brain that was particularly fond of biscuits, cakes, sweets, chocolate, ice cream and pretty much any other sweet yummy loveliness.

My compulsive eating didn't stop there though. I also liked savoury food and devoured more pork pies, sausage rolls, crisps and snacks than anybody else I knew. I loathed myself for this and spent decades hating myself for not being able to control my eating.

There was also something else I found very perplexing. If I was at a function like a wedding, christening or birthday party, if I stayed completely away from the buffet, I was absolutely fine. But the minute I took one mouthful, all hope was lost. I'd hoover up whatever I could lay my hands on – usually till I felt sick.

The reason for this became apparent and was one of the best lightbulb moments I had, when I was diagnosed with ADHD. The reason I could not touch the food but lost all control when I had eaten one mouthful was purely down to my ADHD brain.

As soon as it had one taste of vol au vent – which to my brain was the equivalent of a class A drug – it didn't want to stop. It wouldn't LET me stop. I used to get very embarrassed, going up to buffet tables three or four times, but I just could not stop eating.

At home, I would spend a week or two frantically counting calories and desperately trying to lose weight and then CRUMBLE. I would hit the newsagent and the bakers and spend a lot of money on cakes, crisps, family bags of different sweets and go home and eat them until I felt very ill. Sometimes I could feel the skin on my stomach so extended that it hurt but I still couldn't stop eating. I cannot begin to tell you how much I hated myself for it. This is one of the ways ADHD low self-esteem comes into play. I thought I was absolutely hopeless, useless, a pig, had absolutely no willpower, no self control and was so embarrassed about my ballooning size. But still I couldn't stop.

So if your teenager has any sort of binge eating or compulsive eating problem and for whatever reason cannot be on ADHD medication, I strongly recommend you book them in with a specific eating disorder therapist. They are going to need help with controlling this if they cannot be on ADHD meds.

At the other end of the scale, anorexia nervosa and restricted eating, even to the point of ARFID, is not uncommon with ADHD teenagers. If we remember that anxiety, overthinking, rumination and low self-esteem can very often be going on all at the same time in your teenager's brain, it's not hard to see why it's not a very long journey from there to reducing food intake. A lot of ADHD teenagers have told me that it's the only way they can feel in control of their life, when the rest of their ADHD traits make them feel so out of control.

Body dysmorphia is not uncommon with ADHD teens either. I have met numerous teenagers who have been many stones overweight due to their compulsive eating, started ADHD medication and lost in excess of five stones, but been unable to accept that they now look different. I worked with one client quite long-term on this and it's extremely well-embedded into some teenagers that their appearance is not how they would want it to be. Again, I think you need an expert therapist who works with ADHD and body dysmorphia to really get on top of this one.

Sensory processing disorder can also impact on your teenager's eating habits. A lot of teenagers will avoid certain food because it's too wet, too dry, too crunchy, too soft, too spicy, too bland, they don't like the colour, they don't like the texture or a hundred other reasons.

We can have the most unbelievable reasons for not liking things. One of mine that always makes people incredulous is that I think avocado is disgusting, yet I've never tasted it once! To me it is a revolting colour, looks like green slush and it's not going anywhere near my mouth. Ever.

So if your teenager has some very unusual reasons for avoiding certain food, don't be surprised. They can be extremely illogical like my avocado one is. Illogical it may be, but for me, there's absolutely not a possibility for me to even try avocado.

If your teenager has an eating disorder I totally appreciate this is extremely worrying for parents. Put yourself in the hands of the specialists. If you are in the UK, the NHS has very good eating disorder services and I'm quite sure there are the equivalent in other countries. Privately you can access all sorts of eating disorder specialists. Always make sure it is one who understands ADHD though, or they can do more damage than good.

Top Take-Aways

It's not unusual for an ADHD teenager to have an eating disorder. And don't think this only applies to girls. It very much applies to boys as well. If you even suspect your teen is struggling with any aspect of food intake, seek specialist support as soon as you are aware.

Don't Bother ...

Thinking that they are doing this just to be the centre of attention. That is almost never the case. More often, it is a combination of their ADHD traits giving them an issue around food and an ADHD eating disorder specialist will be able to get on top of this very quickly.

DAMAGE LIMITATION TARGETS:

43
PERIODS – AND HOW GIRLS DON'T NEED TO SUFFER ANYMORE

Hopefully we've all accepted by now that ADHD is a condition connected to hormones? And hormones, as we know, are hugely involved in what goes on in a female ADHD teen's body once a month.

Having worked with lots of ADHD females over the years, I have found that we've all had something in common. And that is we have all had horrible problems with our menstrual cycle.

The first problem we will deal with is pain. ADHD women, including teenagers, seem to have more pain than their non-ADHD counterparts. I know I absolutely dreaded my periods every month. Day one was usually just about okay but come days two, three and four I was often in screaming, writhing agony, in so much pain, I just did not know what to do with myself. Very little seemed to help. Painkillers didn't touch the sides. Hot water bottles only helped marginally. The only thing that did help was going to sleep when often the pain was so bad it made me practically lose consciousness anyway.

The pain was that severe on one occasion a partner of mine called an ambulance. On another occasion, trying desperately to get out of a car after an aborted shopping trip due to the extreme pain, I passed out and fell into the gutter. I was in so much pain I didn't care.

Just about every woman I have spoken to with ADHD has said they have had horrendously painful periods. But thanks to medical advancements since those dark ages, I am now told there is much better pain relief for periods and quite frankly – thank God because I hate to think of anybody else going through such horrendous pain.

Another common theme seems to be length of menstruation. I was relatively lucky in that mine were done and dusted within about six days, but I've met many ADHD women who have told me their periods last for ten or eleven days. The worst was a fortnight. Poor woman. I felt for her. And don't you just want to punch those neurotypicals who say 'oh mine only last two or three days and I barely notice them with no pain whatsoever'. I have never punched anybody, but those people came close!

Various people have told me there are now wonderful medications that reduce flow, stop most of the pain and even eradicate the period itself with the benefit of the contraceptive pill if they are that unbearable. For all the ADHD teenage girls out there, I cannot begin to tell you how happy I am for you.

Something else we also seem to have worse is PMT, as in premenstrual tension. I was never aware of mine, but other people were. I became a snappy, sniping, wound-up, tense viper for about ten days until I suddenly felt – and I mean physically felt – the release in my body. Very difficult to explain but I suddenly felt like a massive wave of relaxation go through my body which actually meant my period was about to start and the premenstrual tension was over. So I never really realised I had the PMT until it was over, but boy did I notice the difference once it went. Happiness returned. Of course that meant the imminent onset of pain, so it wasn't all good.

There are all sorts of medications, both natural and prescribed, you can now take for premenstrual tension, and if your teenager is suffering with this, then I would most definitely let them speak to the GP about it and take whatever help is on offer. There is no need to feel like a snappy dragon for a third of the month anymore.

Some have premenstrual tension so badly it is now classified as premenstrual dysphoric disorder (PMDD). This is when the premenstrual symptoms are even more heightened than mine. And is well worth a google if you think your teenager is having some very severe mood swings before her actual period. Again, there is medication that can help with this now.

Something else which might sound silly, but it's actually very serious. If your teenage daughter is using tampons I strongly suggest she sets alarms on her phone for when to change them. I cannot begin to tell you how many times I had to go to the doctors thinking I had left a tampon in when actually I had taken it out. Our short-term memory can be so bad that we forget if we have put one in or taken one out. And there is nothing more embarrassing than having a doctor forage around 'down there', looking for something that you took out a couple of hours ago.

And again the opposite, leaving a tampon in for far too long. I know of people who have actually permanently affected their ability to have children by leaving a tampon in too long so this is a very serious matter.

Obviously when I was having periods it was way before the time of mobile phones and there was no such luxury as putting an alarm on the phone, reminding me to change after so many hours, but I would certainly use it now.

If your teenager is in school and not able to have their phone during the day, I would try to get them in the habit of changing at lunchtime and again straight after school. It's not too bad when there is a routine, but it's weekends and evenings when it will all go haywire and the reminders on the phone will be useful.

Top Take-Aways

Periods are nearly always going to give your ADHD teenage daughter problems. The minute this happens, ship her straight into the GP and see what the options are to help with whatever issues she is having.

Don't Bother …

Dismissing it as something everybody goes through and she's just got to deal with it.

If she has inherited her ADHD from her dad, and Mum doesn't have ADHD, Mum might not be able to understand just how severe period pain can be for an ADHD daughter. If she tells you she's in screaming agony and she can't cope with it anymore, believe her. And get help.

DAMAGE LIMITATION TARGETS:

44
SEXUAL HEALTH AND THE DREADED STIS

'Sexually transmitted infections' that stands for, for those of you who, like me, wouldn't have had a clue. Wouldn't have had a clue until I contracted one in my mid-50s. I joke not. And this is why I have included it in this book because it was only then I found out that ADHD people have a much higher risk of having sexually transmitted infections! Who knew! I wish somebody had told me this before.

It is all perfectly true though. And when you think about it, it makes sense. We are the people out there risk-taking, thrill-seeking and not thinking of the consequences.

We are also pushing boundaries and doing things impulsively so of course who is going to get caught more often than anybody else for not thinking before and grabbing a handy condom? Yep. ADHD people, and that includes your ADHD teenager.

So while this is never going to be an easy conversation to have, I do suggest you have it, particularly when you know they are dating or at the point of potentially starting a sexual relationship.

I would keep it nice and factual, which is that ADHD people are more at risk of contracting sexually transmitted infections. And if they want to avoid that, their very best plan of action is to have a reliable supply of condoms, and at least one on them at all times. And that's the same advice whether they are male or female.

It really is better than contracting something that, in some cases, you can't get rid of for life. Of course, some of the STIs can be treated usually with antibiotics which gets rid of them, but some of them can't.

So the best way of getting this into your teenager's brain is to tell them that they have the choice. They either use condoms at all times and get themselves checked regularly for sexual health, which usually won't cost a penny OR they risk contracting something possibly even their partner doesn't know THEY have, and that infection could stay with them for life.

It would also mean them having to explain to future partners that they have an STI, which wouldn't be anybody's choice.

So of course it's totally up to them what they do, but you strongly recommend they remember their condition makes them risk-take and thrill-seek more than anybody else and they are going to be doing things impulsively.

Be sure they understand this is not a fault and you are not scaremongering, but it is better to be prepared and to protect themselves as much as they possibly can.

It's worth noting that a condom doesn't protect you from all sexually transmitted infections, but it goes a long way towards it. So if you can only get them using condoms with the occasional sexual health check that's about as good as it gets.

Top Take-Aways

ADHD teenagers and adults are more at risk of contracting a sexually transmitted infection. It's important your teenager knows that and it's up to you to tell them as I doubt anybody else will!

Don't Bother ...

Lecturing them or telling them they have to do this, that, or the other and are stupid if they don't. That won't work.

Just present them with the information, tell them how to best protect themselves and then leave it up to them. Offer to go to the sexual health clinic with them if and when they decide the time is right. They might prefer to go with a mate. Either is fine. Going is the important thing.

DAMAGE LIMITATION TARGETS:

45
GENDER IDENTITY AND SEXUAL PREFERENCES

This is a bit of a fascinating area when it comes to ADHD. A lot of us ADHD therapists have noticed that there tends to be more non-binary, bisexual, pansexual and sexually experimental ADHD people than there are in the neurotypical world.

I'm quite sure everybody has an opinion on why this is the case, but my own is that ADHD people do find 'normal' and 'expected' terribly boring. So experimenting with anything different, and not just sexually, is very common for us. So is this perhaps why we experiment more and are open to new and different sexual ways of looking at/doing things than other people? I strongly suspect so.

I also think it's because we like to risk-take and thrill-seek. And we love pushing boundaries.

I have worked with parent clients who have been absolutely horrified to see their, as far as they knew, perfectly straight child up to sexual activities with their same-sex best friend. This is reasonably common.

And I have worked with clients who have been sexually active from a very young age with brothers or sisters. This is way more common than any of us ever knew. When I investigated it, professionally, I was told 'it is probably going on in every street in the country'. That shocked me, but apparently early sexual experimentation with brothers or sisters is incredibly common.

ADHD teenagers are always looking for something daring, something that will shock other people, something that will stimulate their perpetually adrenaline-seeking brain.

So firstly, I wouldn't be too shocked if your teenager experiments sexually with somebody you are not expecting. Try not to show it! Unless it's a sibling which is a different matter entirely, and never acceptable. There are very specific charitable organisations that specialise in this area and I would strongly recommend you get in touch with one of these – you may even have one very local to you. The very best thing is not to overreact. The more you overreact and judge the more they will push to shock you further and to get a reaction out of you. Remember that 'liking to push boundaries' trait. It's always there.

Also expect them to change their mind. The adolescent years for every teen are all about experimentation, finding out who you are, what you like and where you fit in in the world. For ADHD people, this is more of a struggle than for most, because they are dealing with all the ADHD traits on top. With so many hundreds of thoughts a day flying through your head, knowing exactly who you are and how you identify is much harder when you have ADHD.

So your only role as they go through this is to be non-judgmental and provide them with what we call in counselling 'unconditional positive regard'. Your PRIME concern needs to be for their safety and their happiness. That is always paramount.

But as long as they are safe and not hurting anybody else, then allow them to experiment to find out what they do like and what they don't. And this can go as far as to wondering if they have been born into the right body. We have had many clients who firmly believe they were born into the wrong body and we have helped them explore their thoughts around transitioning – or changing gender.

This can be very painful for parents who have become used to loving their daughter Millie only for her to suddenly become their son Billy. Tough as this is for parents, it is tougher for the teenager going through it, so we always recommend that you book them in with a therapist who understands ADHD and how ADHD teenagers can question their identity and gender. A therapist can also help parents work through their feelings if they are struggling to adjust to the situation.

Top Take-Aways

It's not unusual for ADHD teenagers to question their sexuality or their gender. Support them unconditionally while they make their own explorations. Knowing you are there to support them, unconditionally, will empower them to make the right decisions for themselves rather than for other people.

If you can afford it, an ADHD therapist who specialises in gender and identity will be worth their weight in gold. Both for your child and for you, if you are struggling to get your head round it.

Don't Bother …

Forcing Billy to deny who he really is because you would prefer him to be Millie. This is not only going to destroy Billy's life, but is going to ruin your relationship with him, and almost definitely leave him a tortured soul who is a safeguarding risk to himself.

DAMAGE LIMITATION TARGETS:

46
ALCOHOL – IF IT BECOMES A PROBLEM

Alcohol may or may not crop up in your ADHD teenager's life. If it doesn't feature at all, then you are lucky to have swerved it, but for the parents where it's causing issues we will go into exactly why.

Firstly, if you are the sort of family who have a drinks cabinet or a few bottles of wine regularly hanging around, you can see why a risk-taking, adrenaline-seeking ADHD teenager might be tempted to try some.

Of course we've all heard the horror stories when 'trying it' became drinking three bottles of wine or mixing beer and wine leading to throwing up all over the furniture and your new cream carpet. If this happens with your ADHD child, don't be surprised because alcohol is one of the most easily available 'naughty' and 'risky' things they can get their hands on at home.

It's very common for young ADHD teenagers to try alcohol and if we are lucky it will make them feel so sick and ill it will put them off it for a long time! It did me when I was anxious about my 15th birthday party and spotted my mother's whiskey on the worktop. As I was putting nibbles onto Ritz biscuits, I started to have the odd slurp from the whiskey bottle for the first time in my life.

This saw me missing my entire 15th birthday party because I was throwing up violently in the bathroom and then had to be put to bed. I re-emerged at 1 a.m. to find everybody had gone home. That's the sort of thing that will put your teenager off. I've not touched whiskey since. Importantly, though, if this does happen, don't take the mickey out of them or humiliate them, because all that will make them want to do is drink again to prove you wrong.

However, there are some teens who do like it and even some who would say they need it. I have met many ADHD teenagers who use alcohol to lessen their anxiety. These teenagers literally have to have a couple of nips of vodka before they can go into school as the whole school thing makes them very anxious. And there are those who use it to help them fall asleep. This only leads to waking up in the night, when it's worn off, and horrible dehydration, so is never a good idea.

This is obviously not good. All of these teens hide it from their parents and usually stash their bottles of booze under the bed, so if you suspect your teenager is having a crafty swig of something before school, go and check under their bed!

The main problem with alcohol is it is legal. So, unlike heroin or cocaine, you are likely to find it in a lot of peoples' houses. This means for an ADHD teenager there is easy access and this is not a good thing. ADHD teens are not good with temptation. Their impulsivity, not thinking of the consequences and desire for excitement means any alcohol on display is going to be extremely enticing for them. So the first thing I would say is if you are going to keep alcohol in the house, then lock it away in a cupboard somewhere out of sight.

ADHD teenagers can start dabbling with alcohol from quite a young age. I've literally heard of 8- and 9-year-olds having a swig of their mother's sherry. So really, don't be surprised if you find a very young teenager who has been swiping the odd nip from Dad's whiskey bottle for years before you find out.

It's risky, naughty, banned and they are not supposed to do it. Therefore it becomes exciting. However, alcohol is not good for a young child's body, and depending on how old they are, I would strongly recommend you have a chat with them about it.

If they are above the legal age for drinking but doing it to excess, the talk needs to be around moderation. It needs to be focused on reducing their intake so it is not dangerous. Binge drinking at weekends is also extremely bad for the body, but I can absolutely guarantee your teenager will not have thought of this.

If they are drinking to excess, encourage them to have as many alcohol-free days a week as they possibly can, and also to intersperse each alcoholic drink with a non-alcoholic drink. So a pint of beer followed by a lemonade, followed by a pint of beer, followed by a lemonade. This way they will become full quicker on half the alcohol. Trust me on this one because I learnt this during my addiction training. It really does work. The drinker does not feel denied but will soon become full up and less able to consume any more. Alcohol will always increase their risk-taking and reduce their impulse control, both of which could spell danger.

But if your child is under the legal age for drinking alcohol, then you need to have a much stronger chat. You have to explain how damaging it is to their body, how alcohol has been linked to breast and other cancers, and you need to find something else that will give them the excitement they are looking for.

Often kids will drink alcohol at home because they are bored. So find out the reason underneath the behaviour before you attempt to change it.

If it is anxiety about school then you need to tackle this head-on. What is giving your child anxiety about school? Are they having friendship problems? Are they struggling in classes because of undiagnosed ADHD coexisting conditions or because they are finding it impossible to understand OR interpret instructions and directions? It's highly likely this is something to do with their ADHD and you might have to play detective to find out exactly what.

If they are drinking purely because they are bored and it's something to do, you need to ramp up their after-school and weekend activities so that they aren't bored enough to turn to alcohol. Alcohol is literally a dopamine hit and feeds the teenager's adrenaline. If they are getting this elsewhere, alcohol suddenly becomes the last thing on their mind.

Also whether or not they are on ADHD medication plays a huge part. I have worked with numerous teenagers who have been drinking excessively but when put on the correct medication they literally stopped drinking overnight. So this is another reason for considering medication if your ADHD teenager isn't on it.

It's very difficult for somebody with ADHD, when they are drinking, to moderate it. Because their brain is screaming at them that 'I'm LOVING this dopamine' and 'would like more right now please'. It's very, very difficult to drink alcohol moderately even as an adult – so difficult that I'm practically teetotal now and prefer a milkshake to a martini.

If you do find your teenager drinking, take it very seriously and if necessary you can call in professional help. There are ADHD therapists who specialise in addiction in teens and I would strongly recommend you book in with one of those.

I have worked with adolescents in their late teens who have been seriously heavy binge drinkers, and it has given them a whole range of health problems, including heart attacks, so this is something that you do need to deal with as soon as it arises. Things can so easily and quickly get out of control with an ADHD compulsive brain.

Also, if you have a late teen who has their own car or motorbike, have the conversation with them about how much they are allowed to drink before they get behind the wheel or the handlebars. Hundreds of ADHD teenagers don't think of the consequences of two or three pints before they drive and many of them lose their driving licenses when they've only just got them.

Not to mention the droves who drink and drive before they have even passed their tests! I've met some of them as well. Find out what your teen is drinking and exactly how much they are legally permitted to have before driving. They probably won't have the time or patience to find this out for themselves.

Top Take-Aways

It's not unusual for ADHD teenagers to experiment with alcohol. Expect it and rather than judging them or telling them off, explain to them that this is connected to their ADHD but the damage on their young body really isn't worth it and you need to find a way together for them to not need the adrenaline alcohol gives.

If they are using alcohol to deal with ongoing anxiety issues, it's better to visit the GP with them to see if they will prescribe anti-anxiety meds. These can be life-changing for some ADHD teens when their life is being held back by anxiety.

Don't Bother ...

Ranting and raving and banning them from all alcohol. All this is going to do is make them do it behind your back. Much better is to say you understand why they are doing it and to find different ways of getting them whatever alcohol is giving them.

DAMAGE LIMITATION TARGETS:

47
CANNABIS AND RECREATIONAL DRUGS –
BE READY FOR IT!

This can be an absolute nightmare for some parents of ADHD teenagers, but I don't want you to automatically think they will all start passing round a joint aged 13 and be a full-blown addict by the time they are 14.

There are people like me with moderate-to-severe ADHD, who have never even smoked cigarettes let alone taken any drugs at all – ever. This is largely because when I was young, there was a well publicised and tragic story of a young girl, Leah Betts, who had taken one drug once and died. This was enough to put me off. I always thought I'd be the person who, with my luck, would be the same – I'd take drugs once and drop dead. So I've always avoided them like the plague.

However, there are a lot of ADHD teens who are way more gung-ho and adventurous than me. The vast majority will start with the use of cannabis and then sometimes move onto harder drugs, and it is those we are going to look at here.

Having worked with trillions of young clients, I would say the most likely age your teenager is going to experiment with drugs, if they are going to, is round about 13 or 14. That experiment starts usually with cannabis. And this is nearly always because a friend is using it and has offered them a smoke.

Teenagers with ADHD then find out quickly that cannabis has some very useful effects. Firstly, it calms down their constantly racing brain and also helps them sleep. So it's not difficult to see why they suddenly think this is fantastic and will fight to the death to use it again.

Just briefly, don't undervalue the importance of 'calming down my brain'. It can be absolutely exhausting having ADHD. Your brain is constantly firing thoughts at you and an unmedicated ADHD teen will find it almost impossible to relax, chill or laze around feeling calm and cool like their mates. (The non-ADHD mates of course!) When that has been denied you all your life, and suddenly cannabis allows you to feel like this, you can completely understand why a teenager might want to hang on to that wonderful, chilled, relaxed feeling they've never experienced before. It will be pleasantly shocking to them that it's even possible to feel like this.

Before I was diagnosed and medicated, I was frequently heard saying 'I will never be able to relax until I'm dead'. That gives you an idea of how wound up and manic our brains are all the time. Now I'm on ADHD medication I know what it feels like to be relaxed.

And the other benefit of cannabis helping them get to sleep we've already covered. Getting to sleep can be an absolute nightmare for some ADHD teenagers and I've had hundreds tell me that smoking cannabis later on in the evening is the only way they will ever sleep.

If they have found this magical elixir that gives them BOTH these previously out-of-reach effects, you can understand why they are going to want to carry it on.

If your teenager isn't medicated, and there is no clinical reason why they can't be, and they start using cannabis a lot – now is the time to talk to a paediatrician about getting them on ADHD medication.

If you have heard that urban myth that 'going on ADHD medication can cause them to become drug addicts later in life' please chuck that one in the bin immediately. It really is the polar opposite. By not medicating your child you have much more chance of them turning to illegal drugs than if they are on the correct ADHD meds. The reason for this is the ADHD medication will have the effect of calming down their brain, and it will also stop their compulsive brain from needing more and more. This will lessen, if not eradicate, any interest in pursuing different drugs.

If any professional ever tells you that putting an ADHD teenager on ADHD meds is going to make them more likely to become a drug addict, please put them right, because it could not be further from the truth. There are even some GPs who still believe this because they don't know enough about ADHD.

ADHD meds will also stop their risk-taking, thrill-seeking, pushing boundaries and 'not thinking of the consequences' behaviours. It will also reduce the chances of them doing anything impulsively – like just trying heroin once because 'their friend offered it to them for free'. So there is a much-reduced risk of them turning to drugs once their brain is safely and correctly medicated for ADHD.

By keeping your child unmedicated, you are leaving them wide open to experimenting with anything and everything that will calm down their brain and this is highly likely to be illegal substances.

The last thing you want is your teenager hiding how much cannabis they are using from you. So it might take an awful lot of gritting of teeth, but allowing them to do it at home, very probably in the garden if you don't want your house reeking of it, is actually wise. Just for the short term.

If you don't allow them to do it at home, you run the risk of them doing it in houses where there are other drugs on offer and an inquisitive ADHD brain is going to find it very hard to say no to 'just trying' those.

I can't begin to tell you the amount of parents I've worked with who have absolutely hated the smell of weed and their teenagers using it. But they have put up with them doing it in the garden so they at least know they are safe and not being approached by drug dealers, trying to entice them on to harder drugs. This is one of the most difficult periods parents can go through but I promise you there is light at the end of the tunnel!

Something else you need to be very careful of at this point is that they don't start using their natural ADHD entrepreneurial skills and start either buying enough cannabis to give or sell to their friends, often at no profit, or to friends of friends. This comes as a very big surprise to a lot of parents, but even your teenager giving cannabis to their best mates who they have known since infant school, makes them, in the eyes of the police, a supplier of class B drugs. And if, heaven forbid, they buy enough to sell on to a few classmates, that makes them a drug dealer in the eyes of the law.

This is something I can almost guarantee 99% if not 100% of ADHD teenagers will not have considered, so when it comes to communicating with your teenager, again, a lot of gritting of teeth, but we need to get this information into their head before they find themselves in a police station.

So cannabis use is serious and we do need to deal with it. I have had two clients in the past who had heart attacks due to their excessive use of, initially, cannabis and then cocaine.

We had one ADHD teen client who took so many drugs he nearly died before the paramedics managed to bring him back. And the amount of crimes that teenagers commit when they're out of their heads on cannabis also means we have to do something about this rather than ignoring it.

I strongly suggest you do your research on the impact of using cannabis or any other drugs your child has progressed onto.

Whichever parent or even uncle, aunt, nan, or grandad, is most chilled about their usage, needs to have a private one-to-one chat with them. Make sure it's confidential and tell them that everything you speak about with them stays between you and them. Talk to them about the risks of what they are doing both to their own health and also legally.

Make it absolutely clear you are on their side, not judging them, because you appreciate this is very much connected to their ADHD, but between you, you need to come up with a plan to either much reduce or hopefully eradicate the use of something that really is not doing them any good and is not going to help them in the long-term.

If your teenager agrees to reduce what they are doing, with the aim of stopping it altogether, then that's a win. If they are not on ADHD medication and agree to try it now, then that is also a win.

If they refuse to do either of these things, adamant that they are not doing themselves any harm, and actually would rather you keep your opinions to yourself, it's the time to call in professional help.

There are two ways of doing this. You can either go to the government-funded drugs services, arm yourself with a ton of leaflets and sit with your teenager while you go through them and hope that they will get the message, that what they are doing is both dangerous, illegal and a gateway to much more serious addiction. You might also be able to get them one-to-one or group therapy via these services. There are also some fantastic charities who support parents and siblings and these are well worth contacting if your ADHD teen's drug use is impacting other family members.

The only problem with this is that they aren't ADHD focused, so if you can afford it, your very best option is an ADHD addiction therapist who can work with your child in confidence. These addiction and ADHD specialists are phenomenal at not judging what the ADHD teenager is doing, but working with them to understand exactly the damage they are doing to themselves and how to get off whatever it is they are taking. My team has some terrific and experienced addiction/ADHD therapists so, if this is a real problem for you, please do contact us and we will help.

Top Take-Aways

Most ADHD teenagers will experiment with cannabis. Not all, but most. So, don't be shocked, but know there is a lot of professional advice out there you can access to help you through this patch your teen, along with thousands of others, is going through.

Don't Bother …

Banning them from using it. Punishing them. Accusing them of throwing all the opportunities away you have given them and instead choosing to be a drug addict. All this will do is make them hide it from you and push boundaries further by taking different drugs purely to annoy you.

DAMAGE LIMITATION TARGETS:

48
THAT SCARY MOMENT WHEN THEY DO SOMETHING ILLEGAL

Not every ADHD person will break the law. But a lot will come perilously close, some will only just manage to swerve it by the skin of their teeth and some will do anything and everything to attract the attention of the police, usually as they enter their teens.

It's not even unusual for this to have started younger and ADHD 10-year-olds can be chucking stones at police cars for a laugh and most definitely to get a reaction. But usually it is very early teens when ADHD kids first bring themselves to the attention of the police.

I have seen this with so many teenagers. It's usually when they are quite severely ADHD and are absolutely hellbent on causing as much disruption to their home lives and pushing boundaries as far as they possibly can. They will literally do anything to get attention and don't care who they upset – in fact, the more people the better.

You really have your work cut out with these teenagers, and I strongly recommend you book them in with a good ADHD therapist, who can help them realise that having a criminal record is going to limit their travel options and their career opportunities. This usually brings most ADHD teenagers to an abrupt realisation that this isn't actually what they want. But only if it's done in a very non-judgmental 'it's your choice' kind of way. And it's usually better from a stranger rather than a family member, who they will think is just nagging and moaning as usual.

So what do you need to be looking out for? In almost all cases, stealing is what happens first. This is usually sweets from the sweet shop, vapes, cigarettes and, for the really brave, tracksuits and trainers.

If new clothes or shoes of any kind start appearing and you've genuinely no idea how they've been paid for, don't fall for the 'a friend gave them to me' line. This is extremely unlikely.

And following on from the previous chapter, you need to make absolutely sure this money isn't being earned from supplying or dealing drugs. Your teenager isn't likely to tell you, so you need your very best detective skills honed and ready. Hercule Poirot and Miss Marple combined is the snooping skill level you need here!

Something else that teenagers often find themselves in trouble for, usually very unexpectedly, is from shouting or fighting in public and being accused of affray. It's also very easy to cause criminal damage by accidentally scratching a car or falling over a neighbour's enormous rose bush. Something your teenager thinks is completely innocuous might be construed very differently by a passing police officer.

Building sites also hold huge appeal for ADHD teenagers. The number I have met who have found themselves in trouble from breaking in to building sites at night, jumping on the scaffolding and having a marvellous time – until they are caught by a furious security guard.

Hyperactivity and restlessness, when out and about, can also mean the occasional kicking of a door, car, wall, shop window or any property, which can easily be construed as criminal damage. This will come as a nasty surprise to your teenager, so it is worth having an open chat with them when they are quite young about the sort of things they might do outside of the home that could get them in to trouble. They might be well used to kicking their wardrobe at home and having no repercussions, because you're so used to it being destroyed, that they won't think twice about kicking something in the street. But that might get a very different reaction from a local police officer.

Many years ago, I came across a genuinely lovely boy, aged about 26, in prison. He had received a nine-year sentence for one kick. This is absolutely true. I met him when I was helping at a Family Day in a prison and was really not sure if he was a visiting dad or brother. He didn't look anything faintly like a criminal.

He had been drunk, admittedly, out on a Saturday night, when a friend of his had punched somebody. It was proven that the punch had been the cause of death when the victim fell to the ground. The boy I met had made the mistake of kicking the victim when he had fallen.

The boy who had punched and killed the victim admitted his crime and received a six-year sentence. The boy who had 'only' kicked the victim when he was already on the ground pleaded not guilty to murder. as his legal team advised, but was sentenced to nine years, even though his kick had actually not contributed to the victim's death.

That's the sort of story you need to tell any of your Hyperactive ADHD teens who think it's okay to kick and punch and there won't be any serious consequences. There are so many ADHD boys in prison for one lash-out of hyperactivity that had a horrible consequence.

I met another young man in prison once, aged about 30. He stood out like a sore thumb because, again, he didn't look anything like a criminal. He told me one night a drunken man in a pub was giving his sister a lot of unwanted attention and when, despite several verbal warnings, he would not stop pestering her, this very beautifully spoken, polite and protective brother had punched him, once.

Unfortunately for him, the man fell backwards and cracked his head open on a pub fireplace, so he was now serving six years for attempted murder. My heart broke for him. He was so out of place. As was the boy doing nine years for one kick.

Something else to be wary of. Do explain to your teenagers that they need to be extremely careful what they put in texts and on Instagram, Facebook and any other social media platforms. I've worked with more than one teenager who has been arrested for 'threats to kill' for something that was said or typed without any genuine meaning behind it, but once it had been committed to text and was in the hands of the police, was taken very seriously.

They also need to know that lots and lots of little crimes can add up and although they might seem insignificant, judges lose patience after a while. One of my all-time favourite young offenders committed yet another silly crime and found himself with a sixteen-year sentence because of the build-up of too much prolific petty crime.

And if you find out they are carrying a knife, somehow you need to get them to stop doing that immediately. They are at more risk of being stabbed themselves just by carrying one, and I've worked with more than one teenager who has been arrested for carrying a knife.

Also be very aware of the dark web. Your teen may explore this when they are bored and there's a lot of stuff on there that an ADHD brain is going to find extremely exciting. I've had ADHD teenage clients order drugs and even guns from it.

If your ADHD teenager is getting into trouble with the law, it might go on for years. But I beg you – do not give up on them. The very last thing you want is them going to juvenile prison or a Young Offender Institute. You might think a quick dose of what it's like to be in prison wouldn't do them any harm, but you would be wrong. All that will happen is that they will meet hundreds of criminals and come out a more skilled and knowledgeable offender, with a lot more dodgy friends than when they went in. And with plans to commit the perfect crime next time without getting caught.

So fight your hardest to keep them away from any lawbreaking activities, because I've seen the results of ADHD kids going into prison, and it rarely ends well. More often it ends up with them becoming repeat offenders, or at worst suicidal because they hate themselves and their life so much.

Something to remember if you do find yourself for the first time in the local police station – whether your teen is aged under 18 or older – they are classed as a 'vulnerable adult' due to their ADHD. This means they are entitled to ask for 'an appropriate adult' to be with them at all times.

This can be you. Or another relative. Or the police can provide one if you ask – handy if your teen has nicked a car and pitches up in a police station 200 miles away at four o'clock in the morning. Your teen won't know this is their right but it is.

However, if they do end up with a prison sentence, please don't think it's the end of the world. Heartbreaking and shocking as it will be, there are things they can do to make their time inside worthwhile. And they absolutely can have a good outcome and they can turn their life around. The odds are stacked against them, but it is not impossible. Especially with your full and unwavering support.

The best use of their time inside will be for them to take a vocational course, if it's on offer, and to come out with a skill that leads straight into work.

The most easy ones to obtain inside prison are usually training to be a barber, a chef and in some, a mechanic or gardener. If your teen is bright and has a reasonably long sentence they can even study for a degree inside prison. The Longford Trust Charity are well worth contacting as they sponsor offenders to study degrees inside prison. Gaining a skill they can use on the outside is critical because most, if not all, offenders reoffend when they aren't working and don't have a steady income.

If counselling is available in the prison, encourage your teenager to sign up for it. Speaking to somebody once a week about their feelings, and how they want their life to be on the outside, is hugely worthwhile.

And as for you, write to them as much as you possibly can. Receiving a letter is a huge boost each day when you are in prison. Even if you don't get replies – keep on writing. And send them plenty of stamps or money to buy stamps. Telephone calls are great but letters and emails they can read over and over again. Yes! You can even email into prisons now. It's cheaper, quicker and you can pay for them to reply to you, saving them the cost of a stamp. Have a look on emailaprisoner.com.

Always keep your communications positive – accept that they have made a mistake, but that is in the past, a blip – we all have them – but it does NOT have to map out the rest of their life. If you keep hammering this home – that was their past and all you are now interested in is their future and what they want their life to look like – eventually they will believe you.

If you can get this into their brain, that this really does have to be the last time they find themselves behind bars, you will give them hope. And hope is what they will have least of behind bars.

I've worked with hundreds of young offenders and mostly they don't think they have any choice. They think they have made their choice by offending and now have to live a life of crime. So constantly encouraging them to think about their future and reaffirming that their past does NOT have to define their future is what they need to hear. But they are going to need to hear it over and over again, because they will be beating themselves up badly for making their previous mistakes, however tough and 'hard-man' they are appearing on the outside.

Top Take-Aways

It is not unusual for ADHD teenagers to become well known by the local police. Rather than judging them, make it very clear you understand this is part of their ADHD. You are on their side, you want the very best for their future, and that means finding ways for them to enjoy life and get lots of excitement and adrenaline without involving breaking the law.

Don't Bother ...

Punishing them. Losing your temper, screaming at them, putting them down and threatening to remove gadgets, pocket money or holidays. This will just make them feel worse about themselves and their life.

You need to build them up with positivity rather than knocking them down further with negativity.

DAMAGE LIMITATION TARGETS:

49
LETTING THEM GROW UP

This is one of the hardest things you will have to do with your ADHD teenager, but it's also absolutely critical to get it right for you and for them.

I've seen this numerous times over the years. Parents, especially mums, are often more involved in an ADHD child's whole life than other parents. They will probably have been at the school more trying to explain their child's ADHD, for starters.

They may well have been involved in fighting for months or even years to get an Education, Health and Care Plan (EHCP) for their child. They might have been to numerous meetings with paediatricians, occupational therapists, speech and language therapists, medication reviews not to mention speaking up on their child's behalf at Cubs, Scouts, Guides, sports, drama and youth clubs.

They also may well have spent many years explaining their offspring's ADHD ways of thinking and acting to aunts, uncles, grannies and grandads who still interpret ADHD behaviour as bad behaviour. So as your ADHD teen grows up, taking your foot off the gas is going to be so much harder than for other parents.

You will naturally be terrified that once you do, everything will go horribly wrong, and all your hard work will have been in vain. But unless you get this bit right, you, the hard-working and loving parent who has represented them, pushed for reasonable adjustments for them everywhere, been on their side and battled hard for their rights, will become their punchbag! This will be very shocking, of course, but I can tell you why it will happen.

ADHD teenagers are fiercely independent. They do not like being told what to do and always think they know best. And once puberty hits they just aren't going to want you doing everything for them anymore. From around the age of 12 they are going to feel they are grown up and they do not need parenting anymore. Of course they do. It just needs to be very different parenting. And a micromanaging, constantly in-their-face parent is going to become their nemesis. So unless you want to become their punchbag, you need to change the way you deal with them.

From puberty on it's best to include your teen in all decision-making concerning them. They genuinely will feel from the age of 12 or 13 they are now grown up and don't want a parent making all the decisions for them. So start to treat them like a young adult as soon as they hit their teens, and make sure that all decisions are made collaboratively. Telling them what to do and making decisions for them is the one thing that is going to wind them up mercilessly. If you speak to them as though they are in charge and their decision matters hugely, you won't go far wrong.

Communication is key. Keep it open and keep it collaborative. They need to know that you accept they are growing up now they have entered their teenage years and they do have the right to have opinions on their own life. The more responsibility you give them, the more responsible they will be. A lot of parents find it very hard to accept this when their teenager has done nothing but disobey them most of their life, but as they are growing up you will start to see the more responsibility you give them, the more grown up they honestly will behave. Hard to believe, but try it.

And don't forget the small stuff. The teenager I worked with who was livid because his mother would not knock before she came into his bedroom? She didn't see why she should because it was her house and she should be able to go where she wanted. But for him, this was a major issue. He wanted his privacy. So if this is important to your child then make sure you knock. There needs to be compromise from now on because your teenager will have strong opinions on just about everything.

Don't expect all things to stay the same. Your pubescent teenager is not going to be the same as their 9-year-old self. Their brains and their bodies are changing dramatically and parents who expect everything to stay the same are always bitterly disappointed. One despondent mum recently told me when her son was 10 he would happily help her unpack the shopping from the car, but now he is 12 he just tells her to f*ck off. Well there's a surprise!

You need to adapt as your teenager grows and changes, they will develop their own personality and their own character. I can't begin to tell you how many parents I've worked with who hark back to the past, reminisce about how the child used to be and think the teenager should be behaving the same way. You really can throw that theory out the window.

An ADHD teenager is very different to an ADHD child. And begging and pleading with them to behave how they did when they were 8 is not going to wash now they are 13.

As I said at the start, this is probably the hardest thing for the parent of an ADHD child to do but if you want a good relationship with your ADHD adolescent, it's crucial you get this bit right.

If you are really struggling with this, enlist the help of a good therapist, one who can work with your child to find out exactly what is driving them nuts at home and at school, and then have sessions with the parents to try to come up with something that collaboratively suits both parties. You might not need to go as far as family mediation, but sometimes that's helpful – especially when siblings are involved and the whole household is in meltdown.

I personally have found a therapy session with a teenager where they get all their gripes and moans OUT and then a second session with the parents, coming up with different ways of saying and doing things, is all that's needed. Incredibly simple but very powerful.

Top Take-Aways

Accept that your ADHD teenager is not the same person as your ADHD child was. Get to know the new version of them. Communicate and collaborate on how things will change as they get older. Listen and hear what they say. Their biggest gripe is always not being listened to and not being taken seriously.

Don't Bother ...

Asking them to behave as they always have done. Reminding them what a delightful 8-year-old they were. That is now irrelevant. They don't need frequent reminders of what a little gem they were when they were 7.

DAMAGE LIMITATION TARGETS:

50
WHEN THEY LEAVE HOME – OR
SOMETIMES DON'T!

This is a very important time for your teenager, and also potentially when things can start to go horribly wrong.

Of course they might not. Your teenager might be mature and grounded, get a good job, share a beautiful flat, have no addiction issues and be living the dream. She or he is highly likely to be an

ADHD teenager who is medicated and won't be giving you much trouble. However, we will talk about the ones who aren't quite so mature and well adjusted, because they need more help.

Firstly, your teenager may have no desire to leave home. My Inattentive ADHD brother was quite content to stay at home, until my mother, exasperated, forced him out of the door aged 28. I on the other hand was racing out of that same door as soon as I was 18, desperate to be in control of my own life.

It's not unusual for some ADHD people, especially boys, to not want to leave home. Why on earth would they? If Mum is still happy to cook, clean, wash their clothes and feed them it's very easy to see why ADHD boys in particular like staying at home.

I know of ADHD adults who are still at home in their 30s, 40s and 50s, and this is often because they don't feel they are able to function in the world on their own. The whole thought of paying bills, rent or mortgages, shopping, cooking, feeding themselves and generally managing as an adult is far too scary and overwhelming for a lot of ADHD adults.

However, if you have an adventurous, independent one who is keen to move into a shared flat or house, then you need to be on your guard, as things could go haywire even if your teen has the best of intentions.

For me at 17, going into London to work and having access to a very good sandwich shop at lunchtime meant my binge eating went completely out of control. I probably put on about three stone in the first three months as I devoured two rounds of sandwiches, crisps and cakes every lunchtime and yet more food on the train home. And that was before my dinner! For other teenagers this is often when alcohol and drugs are suddenly freely available and become a problem. Sometimes a very serious problem.

So do keep a good lookout for your teenager as they get more freedom because, more than neurotypicals, they will relish this freedom and often take things to excess.

Money will often be a problem at this point in their life. They may well be managing it on their own for the first time and certainly when I was 18 I was sent a huge amount of letters by credit card companies offering me credit. I of course took all of them up on it and then spent my entire 20's in very bad debt. I think credit card companies are better about this now but be aware of your teenager being offered credit by anybody as it's going to be very hard for them to say no.

I suggest your new role is very much as a non-judgmental, fully supportive and understanding parent!

Again, there might have to be a lot of gritting of teeth, but your teenager needs to make mistakes so they learn from them. The worst thing a parent can do at this stage is do everything for their teenager. I've seen this happen and all you end up with is a scared, incompetent and ultimately angry person in their early 20s who cannot function as an adult because their parents took over and did absolutely everything for them. So I strongly recommend you take up a supportive role, but not an 'oh I'll do it for you' one.

If they invite you round to their shared flat, even if you are horrified at the way they are living, try not to judge. And if your teenager is staying up till all hours, binge-watching television, eating rubbish, leaving the washing up for a month and generally living like a pig, smile sweetly, and say nothing. This will change, but not by you chastising them for it, nor by you doing it for them.

Treat your teenager as an adult. Invite them out for a curry, round to the house for Sunday lunch or for cappuccino and cake in a coffee shop. And that is your time for finding out what is going on in their life in a very casual manner!

For the best outcome, when a teenager is finding their feet in the adult world, your role is to be a fully supportive parent offering unconditional positive acceptance, no matter what your teenager has been up to – unless of course it involves addiction or criminal activities when I do suggest you get involved.

Understand that their ADHD traits mean they are going to get into more pickles and trouble than others their own age. This is part of their condition and it will frustrate them just as much as it does you, if not more. But having a parent who is there supporting them, no matter what, and always keeping the lines of communication open is definitely the best way to manage this.

If you inadvertently slip into being judgmental and chastising them for what their ADHD has naturally got them into, they will close down and not tell you what is actually going on in their life. This is not what you want.

Top Take-Aways

You now need to treat your teen like an adult. Be supportive, non-judgmental, helpful and give advice when it is asked for.

Expect blips. When they happen use them as a learning experience and encourage your teen to think for themselves how they will choose to do things differently next time.

Don't Bother ...

Taking over because they are making such a mess of things, or telling them what to do. They will rebel even more. Be non-judgmental and supportive and know you've done your best to set your own ADHD teenager up for life.

DAMAGE LIMITATION TARGETS:

51
WHAT ONE OF MY TEENAGE EX-CLIENTS – NOW AGED 20 – WOULD LIKE YOU TO KNOW

He knows he is hard work, and when his parents advise him, he wants it to be helpful rather than making him feel small.

If people treat him with respect, he will respect them back.

He cannot tolerate being belittled or intimidated, especially by teachers. When he was eight and nine, he felt he was picked on by teachers who really didn't like him and it has stayed with him. He cannot cope with criticism, people being patronising, or anybody screaming at him that he is wrong.

The message he always got from teachers and friends was that he wasn't good enough, he wasn't doing it right, and he didn't fit in.

He was made to sit at the front of the class, which he absolutely hated.

He has never felt he could be himself. He didn't like adhd medications, although he did try them.

He always feels he has got something to prove – that he is not weak, and although he can appear to be confident, inside he is not confident. On the outside, he is loud, cocky and arrogant, but if he is rude to somebody he will beat himself up for days afterwards, feeling bad.

Being listened to is massively important and the tone of somebody's voice is very important. It will completely affect how he will react. He does not want to be patronised or humiliated. He wants support and understanding.

He knows he can be wound up very easily by children, adults and teachers. He thinks people know they will get a reaction out of him and do it on purpose.

He knows he doesn't learn from his mistakes and doesn't need this pointing out to him.

Only his mum and nan always told him he was special and had potential. They made him believe in himself. He loves people who make the effort to understand him. He knows he comes from a good family, but this hasn't stopped him going off the rails at times.

His mum always had firm boundaries. He respected her for that.

Being told to turn the other cheek doesn't work. His heightened sense of justice will always get in the way.

He knows every day what he gets wrong, 100% of it and knows that his adhd brings him more obstacles, but he will still not give up.

From the age of 13 to 16, he always desperately wanted money. He wanted holidays – to exciting places. Not boring places.

He feels like he has been walking around with chains on all his life and believes that because he is different people always have things to say to him. He feels he has always had to conform to fit in.

When he is angry, his rage boils over, and there is nothing he can do about it. He feels that adults devalue the intensity of his emotions.

He knows at times he has scared his family with his anger. He doesn't want to. He feels terrible afterwards.

James, 20

Now training to be a professional boxer

52
BEFORE I LET YOU GO

And that's it! That's everything I know to help your teenager get through their adolescence undamaged.

Firstly, thank you so much from the bottom of my heart for wanting to understand your ADHD teenager better. I am absolutely passionate about these kids. I adore every single one of them I have ever met. They are feisty, opinionated, don't take no for an answer and have such grit and determination.

Yet, as you have seen by reading this book, they are dealing with a hell of a lot more than most people. Their ADHD alone brings so much with it, never mind what other coexisting conditions they might have. But still they battle on with good humour, knowing that they will always bloody well win, no matter what life throws at them. These are some of the most incredible teenagers you will ever meet.

And don't forget these feisty 'know it all' teenagers are going to turn into world leaders, stadium-filling comedians, Hollywood actors, pop stars, sporting gold medallists and entrepreneurs. They just aren't ever going to come second because coming second is losing for ADHD people, so your teen is a winner.

Winners aren't always easy to parent. Of course they aren't. Because they know best from a very young age and also want their own way from a very young age, but if you get the parenting bit right, these teenagers will absolutely fly.

Three of my all-time favourite teen private clients had all been arrested for some quite serious stuff when I met them. One is now training to be a lawyer, determined to help ADHD people in trouble; one is in his final year at university, training to work professionally in the football world, and the other one is almost a fully qualified doctor. They had parents who believed in them and I believed in them as well. I pushed them to make the best of themselves, and although between them they had very severe ADHD, ASD, dyspraxia, dyslexia, dysgraphia, sensory processing disorder and other issues, ALL of them have pushed through and they WILL win at life because their parents had the good sense to put them in front of an ADHD coach, and I was lucky enough they chose me.

If you are dealing with the most angry, vile, irritable, miserable, 'I hate everyone and everything' teenager – don't lose hope. Because that was me. I hated the world all through my teens and then I turned into a counsellor and now I adore pretty much everybody. Especially if they have ADHD, because they are much more interesting and usually funny.

Parents who have lost all hope with their teenagers, have been staggered by the change when they reach their early 20s. Once out of puberty, they will become a completely different person and I guarantee you will like them a lot more!

Nobody is saying that parenting an ADHD teenager is easy. In fact it has to be one of the hardest jobs there is, but if you do it right you will be launching an ADHD adult into the world who is probably going to make a difference somehow. Yes, it's going to be rocky at times but it always is when ADHD is involved.

I urge you to love them with a passion. And let them know that you love them with a passion, despite whatever troubles their ADHD traits get them into.

Always push them to be their best self and instil in them the knowledge that ADHD gives them the power to achieve more than anybody else.

So I wish you the very best of luck with your ADHD teenager. I truly hope this book has helped you in some way. And, don't forget, we have a very large team of ADHD counsellors, addiction therapists and coaches at the ready if you need that extra bit of support. There's more information at the back of the book on those.

You are not alone. There are thousands of parents worldwide parenting ADHD teenagers right now. And there are a lot of times when you are going to think you've got it wrong. But just keep doing your best because you have a very special person in your hands who is going to go on to do great things. You just need to get them through these teenage years, which really are the most difficult of their lives. Then – I absolutely promise you – everything gets a lot better!

With the biggest amount of ADHD love I can possibly send you,

Sarah

Summer 2023

WHO I NEED TO THANK

Here we go. The bit that bores people to death, but there are some people I really ought to thank, bearing in mind this is the third book I've written on ADHD and I haven't thanked anybody so far!

Taking into account it wasn't even my idea to write a book in the first place, the thanks for that has to go to Ruth, who didn't listen to my protestations of being 'far too busy seeing hundreds of ADHD clients to write a book' and forced me to get everything out of my brain and onto paper. I will never be able to thank her enough. Meeting somebody standing on the X as an extra for a Halifax advert in the 1990s, has to be one of the most random ways of making a friend.

Then there are my incredible Book Team:

Sophie, who makes sense of and collates all my random chapters, dictated onto an iPhone due to me being a technical no-go area. She also battles Amazon, who really ought to do something about their customer service, because it is shocking. It's a wonder the poor girl hasn't had a breakdown dealing with their non-existent seller support. Sophie is nothing short of amazing and I would be lost without her.

Louise, who is newest to the team but deals with all the book wholesalers, eBay book orders, and anything else I throw at her on a daily basis.

Olli, the publisher, who then became not-my-publisher when it all kicked off on Twitter over the title of my first book. An absolute fount of publishing knowledge, always ready to advise, and still helps me with all the boring bits like typesetting and formatting, which my dyscalculic brain isn't faintly interested in. A true diamond.

Sarah Dawes, the editor, who puts up a good fight when I refuse to listen to most of her amendments. Because obviously being ADHD I know best. But without her we would be lost. And definitely a lot less professional!

Yet another Sarah. This time Sarah Scott, who has designed the cartoons for all three books. Believe it or not, we've still not met, with her living in the wilds of the north-east! But being a qualified graphic designer with the same sense of humour as me, we have a riot doing the cartoons for every book, and some readers say the cartoons are their favourite part. Sarah – please never leave me. The books will not be the same without your cartoons. Two words. Erect Slinkies!

The social media team, headed up by my phenomenal and staggeringly creative niece Isabel – or Issybells to me – ably assisted by Becky who comes up with all sorts of innovative ways of posting the books on Facebook.

Becky also deserves a special mention for flying out to Rhodes and spending a week with me making sure I hadn't missed out anything crucial, her having two, possibly three, ADHD teenagers of her own. Slogging through every chapter, she was determined we didn't miss anything out as, like me, she is passionate about ADHD teenagers.

Phil and Clare, 'the website people'. Clare also designs the covers of the books. The most supportive and helpful IT team it's possible to have. We keep them busy because things keep changing and getting bigger and better but without these two absolute stars we would be in a technical desert.

Michele, who has the unenviable job of keeping on top of the Headstuff email inbox as well as dealing with all our new therapists. She has the patience of a saint and is the only non-ADHD member of the team. We trained as counsellors together and I liked her from the very first day I met her. So glad she's still with us.

Sindy Smith, who tries her level best to control me, never succeeds, but does a wonderful job of looking after all our fabulous Headstuff counsellors. Without Sindy, everything would grind to a halt. We've both come a long way since meeting when we were 8 and 10, when neither of us had any clue we were both ADHD. She's simply amazing.

And while we're on the subject …

My totally amazing team of Headstuff ADHD counsellors and coaches. Without them I would still be in my therapy room working with hundreds of ADHD clients. But these fabulous therapists I do trust with my precious clients, because they are all SO good and like me, they genuinely care and will go the extra mile to help ADHD people. You are ALL the best and I'm grateful to you all.

To the ADHD Liberty team – thank you for being as passionate as me about changing the ADHD world, particularly the criminal justice system and the education system. Alex, Daley, Sean and Colin: I'm proud to know and work with every one of you.

In this list should be Guy – The Print Guy. Guy printed both the first and second books and dealt patiently with our ADHD random requests, changes of plans, last-minute dramas and was an absolute angel. Tragically Guy is now an actual angel, having lost his life to cancer just as this book was being finished. Guy, we all thank you. You were part of this journey and you will never be forgotten.

Now comes that bloody awful moment when I rack my brains, terrified I have missed anybody crucial out.

I don't think I have, so the biggest love and thanks EVER to all of you. Together we WILL improve the lives of ADHD kids and adults and because we are ADHD, we won't ever give up and we WILL bloody well win!!!!!!

ADDITIONAL RESOURCES

Sarah's other books and websites, which might be of help to you:

HeadstuffADHDTherapy.co.uk

Fully qualified ADHD counsellors, children's counsellors, family mediators, coaches and addiction therapists, all diagnosed ADHD themselves. Based in the UK but working internationally.

Provides ADHD training for schools, the criminal justice system, businesses and charities.

How NOT to Murder your ADHD Kid: Instead Learn How To Be Your Child's Own ADHD Coach!

Sarah's first book on parenting younger ADHD kids.

Teachers! How Not to Kill the Spirit in Your ADHD Kids –
Instead, Understand their Brains and Turbocharge our Future
Leaders & Winners

A book written to help teachers understand ADHD children's brains. If you are struggling to have your child understood at school, this book should help.

ADHDLiberty.org

If your child is struggling with addiction or offending behaviour, or if you want to get involved in campaigning for the rights of ADHD children and adults.

SarahTempleton.org.uk

Sarah is a passionate advocate for urgent ADHD screening, recognition and acceptance especially in the criminal justice system and the education system.

She is available for interviews, articles, podcasts, public speaking and keynote speaking.

And books from other authors:

Delivered From Distraction

by Edward M Hallowell MD and John J Ratey MD, Ballantine Books 2005, ISBN: 9780345442314

For adolescents/adults with ADHD or wanting to know more about adult ADHD. A brilliant book written by a psychiatrist with ADHD himself. Really easy to read even for those of us who can't concentrate to read books! Funny, incredibly informative and highly recommended. I always say to the teens and adults I work with, 'If you buy only one book on ADHD, make it this one.'

The ADHD Effect on Marriage

by Melissa Orlov, Specialty Press/A.D.D. Warehouse 2010, ISBN: 9781886941977

A fabulous book if your relationship is running into trouble because either one or both of you are ADHD. Doesn't just work for married couples. Also brilliant for people in new relationships when one or other is ADHD. Really helps you understand how the ADHD traits impact on relationships and best ways of rectifying things.

Taking Charge of Adult ADHD

by Russell Barkley PhD, The Guildford Press 2010, ISBN: 9781606233382

This is a great book for teenagers and adults alike. Goes into lots of detail about ADHD and importantly gives you tons of different ways of overcoming individual traits. Really easy to read book and very useful tips.

Smart But Stuck

by Thomas E Brown PhD, Jossey Bass 2014, ISBN: 9781118279281

This is an easy read, with some excellent strategies for children and adolescents who are getting stuck for whatever reason. Purely using case studies of teens he has worked with, it gives different ways of overcoming 'stuckness' from different ADHD traits such as lack of motivation, procrastination, perfectionism, inability to make a decision and more.

Printed in Great Britain
by Amazon

59142589R00165